Math and Music

Harmonious Connections

Trudi Hammel Garland
and Charity Vaughan Kahn

Dale Seymour Publications

The authors and publisher gratefully acknowledge permission to reprint the following copyrighted material:

Pages 3, 113, 114, and 118: buffaloes, Norway spruce, proportion illustration, and violin, by Shirley Nootbaar. *Page 68*: "Infinity Circle." From *Inversions*, copyright 1989 Scott Kim. *Pages 77–78*: Twelve-note tone rows. Reprinted with permission from *Applications of Secondary School Mathematics, Readings from the Mathematics Teacher*, copyright 1991 by the National Council of Teachers of Mathematics. *Page 79*: Fugue II by J. S. Bach. Copyright by the Associated Board of the Royal Schools of Music, London. *Pages 97 and 100*: Three antique woodcuts of Pythagoras. From *Physics and Music* by Harvey E. White and Donald H. White, copyright © 1980 by Saunders College Publishing, reproduced by permission of the publisher. *Page 102*: Boethius, Pythagoras, Plato, and Nicomachus. From *A History of Mathematics*, Carl B. Boyer, copyright © 1968, reprinted by permission of John Wiley & Sons, Inc. *Page 109*: Photograph of Einstein's house. Erich Lessing/Art Resource, NY. *Page 115*: Analysis of Bartok music. Adapted with permission from Erno Lendvai, *Bela Bartok, An Analysis of His Music*, 28, 29. Published by Kahn and Averill, London, England. *Page 117*: Examples of Fibonacci intervals between notes. Copyright © 1941, 1942, 1946 by Carl Fischer, Inc., New York. Copyrights renewed. All rights reserved. International copyright secured. *Pages 129–131 and 134–135*. White, 1/*f*, and Brownian noise; and white, brown, and 1/*f* music. © 1978 Richard F. Voss/IBM Research.

Project Editor: KATARINA STENSTEDT
Production/Mfg. Coordinator: CLAIRE FLAHERTY
Design Manager: JEFF KELLY
Composition: MANSFIELD MUSIC GRAPHICS
Illustrations: JANET SMITH
Text and Cover Design: LISA RAINE
Cover Image: © TELEGRAPH COLOUR LIBRARY/FPG INTERNATIONAL

Dale
Seymour
Publications

Pearson Learning Group

ISBN 0-86651-829-0
Printed in the United States of America
18 19 20 21 22 V036 12 11 10

1-800-321-3106
www.pearsonlearning.com

To Kit Wilson
for her wisdom,
cheerfulness,
and generous spirit.

We would like to express appreciation to our colleagues and students at the Head-Royce School in Oakland, California, whose interest in and enthusiasm for math and music helped enormously in the development of this manuscript.

Individuals for whose contributions we are especially grateful include Nancy Knop, Shirley Nootbaar, Bill Ludke, Barbara Anderson, Ilene Holmgren, and members of the staff of Dale Seymour Publications.

On a personal level, we wish to express our gratitude to Bruce Garland, Hertha Hammel, Bob and Garda Kahn, Chandra Hampson, Elicia David, Steve Miller, Kay Drengler, Stevie Kaplan, and Sam Johnston for their inspiration, patient encouragement, and loving support.

Contents

THE ESSENCE

PICTURE THE ROCKY shore of a Northern California beach. It is dawn, and the tide is high. The waves roll in and out, in and out, splashing hypnotically over the rocks as the tide drifts deliberately seaward. The sun rises, traversing the spectrum from indigo to mauve to vibrant orange, and creeps slowly across a sky filled with pulsing wind and wildly changing clouds. The tide returns with the sunset, and the moon and stars begin their travels overhead. As the seasons pass by, the rugged shore will erode and change. Plants, animals, fish, birds, and insects will be born, grow, migrate, and die.

All of this is part of the vast, delicate, interconnected web called the universe—a system filled with patterns, rhythms, and cycles. Some are external to us, such as the seasons, the weather, and the tides; others are internal, such as our heartbeats, dream cycles, and hunger pangs.

A phenomenon called **resonance** occurs when two sources of vibration beating out similar cycles are placed in close enough proximity that they begin to pulse at the same rate. There are many instances in nature where different rhythms or cycles begin to beat together, or **entrain**. Fireflies synchronize their flashes of light, frogs croak in time, and women living in the same quarters often begin to menstruate on the same cycle.

The existence of all these patterns and rhythms lends some insight into the connections between two seemingly disparate subjects: mathematics and music. While mathematics is used to explain the patterns and rhythms of the universe, music helps us entrain with these patterns. The musician—composer, performer, or listener—entrains his or her own internal rhythms, mental or physical, with the larger, external rhythms. The rhythm of music is like a heartbeat that connects all beings to one another and to the cycles of the universe.

It's not surprising that one can get the same feeling when appreciating a colorful sunset or a massive redwood tree, when learning and understanding a particularly elegant mathematical theorem, and when listening to Bach's six *Brandenburg Concertos*. It is a feeling of experiencing something pure, beautiful, and somehow perfect, a feeling that these separate experiences are connected at some profound and deep level.

To more easily appreciate the connections between math and music, it is helpful to look back to a time when nature's rhythms were still recognized and revered, when people were just beginning to develop the concept of number and to count, when they discovered that hitting two sticks together repeatedly made a pleasing sound. Without delving too deeply into the origins of either discipline in various cultures, let's see what interesting connections we can find.

Humans have been playing music and making rhythm for ages. There is anthropological evidence that music, in the form of chanting, came before speech. In order to chant, one only needs lungs and vocal chords, conditions that archaeologists have found to exist in skeletal remains that are 580,000 years old. In order to speak, one also needs considerable dexterity of mouth and tongue, developments that didn't occur until much later, about 80,000 years ago.

Curiosity about sound and different ways to create it most likely led to the invention of musical instruments other than the voice. Unfortunately, because many early instruments were probably made of wood, gut, reed, horn, or other materials that readily decompose, we may never know how long ago the first note was sounded.

The oldest evidence found is from Siberia and dates back 35,000 years—before the last ice age. Archaeologists found a group of mammoth bones, including the very large hip and shoulder joints, that had been used as drums. They were marked at the spots that produced the best sounds when struck. Also found were a beater, or drumstick, and two small flutes, all carved out of bone.

At the time when ancient peoples were making music with these primitive instruments, they were of necessity in tune with the natural rhythms of the universe. In hunter-gatherer societies, people had to understand the cycles of migrating herds and know when the nuts and berries would be ready to eat. Later, when agriculture was developed and people began to settle in one place in order to grow crops, they became even more dependent on the natural rhythms of the seasons and the weather.

Although industrialization has served to continually distance people in modern times from the rhythms of the natural environment, rhythm is still an integral part of daily life in many parts of the world. Mothers in many cultures carry their babies in slings close to their bodies so the infants can learn the rhythms of heartbeat and movement. In Southeast Asia, children are taught to dance to the rhythms of music as soon as they can walk. These rhythms are as much a part of them as the food, religion, and customs of the culture. And in many areas of Africa, children drum from early on because the people believe that to lead a proper life, one must be in tune with all surrounding rhythms. An old African proverb reads, "A village without music is a dead place."[1]

How does being in tune with rhythm relate to mathematics? Perhaps the most basic connection is that the timing of the beat of a rhythm is mathematical in nature. But mathematics can also be used to explain why some notes sound higher than others, why instruments are tuned the way they are, and why some sounds are more "musical" than others. Composers use mathematics in subtle ways to create musical compositions that have sufficient unity and structure to be pleasing and to endure. Finally, mathematics is useful in documenting and understanding the music of many diverse cultures through the ages.

This is not to say that all music can be reduced to some final mathematical equation. If this were so, it would be possible to program a computer to create and play music with the same feeling, expression, intensity, and spontaneity as can a human musician. Not every musician thinks about the mathematics involved in his or her composition, performance, or listening experience. After all, the complicated math and physics needed to explain the properties of a musical tone are not understood by everyone, and yet people of all ages and of every culture are able to create and enjoy music.

Music is universal, crosses cultural, historical, and intellectual boundaries, and is grounded in mathematics. Mathematics is also universal, crosses cultural, historical, and intellectual boundaries, and is reflected in music. The interconnectedness of math and music pulsates and sings with a rhythm and harmony of its own.

CHAPTER 2

THE BEAT

THE STORY OF the connections between math and music necessarily begins with **rhythm**. Rhythm is the basis upon which music is built, just as the concept of number is the basis of mathematics.

Rhythm is created whenever the time continuum is split up into pieces by some sound or movement. Waves crashing onto the shore at the beach create a rhythm, as does the beating of your heart, the methodical blinking of the traffic light at the corner, and countless other happenings in the natural and humanmade worlds.

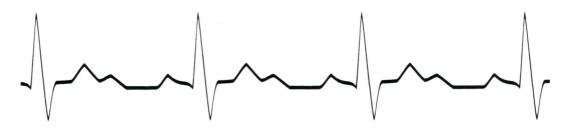

Some of these rhythms are soothing, some are jarring, and some make us want to get up and dance. Rhythm is the life of music, and the rhythms found in music around the world are almost as varied as the rhythms of nature, which may have been the original models.

In order to talk about rhythm and its relationship to number, it is necessary to introduce some vocabulary and notation. These words and symbols are part of a theory of music used today mostly in Western cultures. People began developing this music theory about 2500 years ago, when they decided it would be useful to have a written notation to record their music. The theory has gone through many changes and is still evolving. Not everyone uses this theory to create a written record of their music. People in many cultures around the world still operate with an oral tradition, passing their music down from generation to generation without writing it down. However, we can still use this theory to explore, if not always to fully explain, the music of other cultures and eras.

Since rhythm measures time, music theory uses the **measure** and the **time signature** to set up the rules of rhythm for a particular piece of music. A piece is divided into equal **measures**, or bars, each of which represents the same amount of time. Within each measure there is a further splitting of time into equal portions, or **beats**.

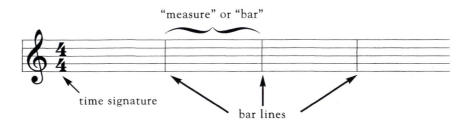

The **time signature** appears at the very beginning of the piece and resembles a fraction. The top number (like the "numerator") tells how many beats of equal length occur in a measure. The bottom number (like the "denominator") tells what kind of **note** gets one beat. There are many kinds of notes; each takes up a different amount of time. This allows for a variety of rhythms that divide time in some very interesting ways. The time signature $\frac{4}{4}$ (or "four four") is the basis for naming the kinds of notes. When a whole measure with a time signature of $\frac{4}{4}$ is filled up with one note, that note is called a **whole note**. If the measure is split into two equal parts, or halves, a note sustained for half of the measure is called a **half note**. Likewise, if the measure is divided into fourths, a note that takes up one quarter of the measure is called a **quarter note**.

Following this pattern, each successive power of two provides a new note to work with—sixteenth notes, thirty-second notes, sixty-fourth notes, and so on. The pattern works the same way for spaces, or **rests**, in the rhythm. A rest that lasts as long as a whole note is a **whole rest**, a **half rest** is equal in time to a half note, and so on.

Name	whole	half	quarter	eighth	sixteenth	etc.
Fraction of Measure	$\frac{1}{1}$	$\frac{1}{2}$	$\frac{1}{4}$	$\frac{1}{8}$	$\frac{1}{16}$	etc.
Number that fit in one measure	$1 = 2^0$	$2 = 2^1$	$4 = 2^2$	$8 = 2^3$	$16 = 2^4$	etc.
Note symbol	𝅝	𝅗𝅥	𝅘𝅥	𝅘𝅥𝅮	𝅘𝅥𝅯	etc.
Rest symbol	▬	▬	𝄽	𝄾	𝄿	etc.

Adding a dot after any note increases its length by one half, creating, for example, a **dotted half note** or a **dotted quarter note**. This method also applies to rests.

$\text{\musicalsymbol} = \text{\musicalsymbol} + \text{\musicalsymbol} = $ dotted half note

$\text{\musicalsymbol} = \text{\musicalsymbol} + \text{\musicalsymbol} = $ dotted half rest

$$\frac{1}{2} + \left(\frac{1}{2} \text{ of } \frac{1}{2} \right) = \frac{1}{2} + \frac{1}{4} = \frac{3}{4} \quad \text{(takes up } \frac{3}{4} \text{ of the measure)}$$

$\text{\musicalsymbol} = \text{\musicalsymbol} + \text{\musicalsymbol} = $ dotted quarter note

$\text{\musicalsymbol} = \text{\musicalsymbol} + \text{\musicalsymbol} = $ dotted quarter rest

$$\frac{1}{4} + \left(\frac{1}{2} \text{ of } \frac{1}{4} \right) = \frac{1}{4} + \frac{1}{8} = \frac{3}{8} \quad \text{(takes up } \frac{3}{8} \text{ of the measure)}$$

All of these notes and rests can be combined in various arrangements to create different rhythms. The only condition is that there must be the same number of beats in each measure.

In a time signature of $\frac{4}{4}$, the top number, 4, indicates that there are four beats of equal length per measure. The bottom number, also 4, tells which note gets one of these beats. Think of a time signature as being like a fraction. In a fraction, a denominator of 4 implies division by 4, which is the same as multiplying by one fourth, or by one quarter. Therefore, the note that "gets the beat" in $\frac{4}{4}$ time is a quarter note.

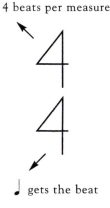

4 beats per measure

♩ gets the beat

So a time signature of $\frac{4}{4}$ states that every measure must contain, altogether, the equivalent of four quarter notes. Using the fraction analogy, the sum of the fractions that each individual note represents must always be 1, because 4/4 = 1. Here are some examples of measures in $\frac{4}{4}$ time that do and don't work out:

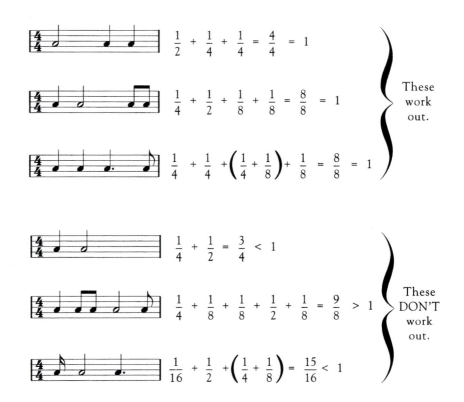

$$\frac{1}{2} + \frac{1}{4} + \frac{1}{4} = \frac{4}{4} = 1$$

$$\frac{1}{4} + \frac{1}{2} + \frac{1}{8} + \frac{1}{8} = \frac{8}{8} = 1$$

$$\frac{1}{4} + \frac{1}{4} + \left(\frac{1}{4} + \frac{1}{8}\right) + \frac{1}{8} = \frac{8}{8} = 1$$

These work out.

$$\frac{1}{4} + \frac{1}{2} = \frac{3}{4} < 1$$

$$\frac{1}{4} + \frac{1}{8} + \frac{1}{8} + \frac{1}{2} + \frac{1}{8} = \frac{9}{8} > 1$$

$$\frac{1}{16} + \frac{1}{2} + \left(\frac{1}{4} + \frac{1}{8}\right) = \frac{15}{16} < 1$$

These DON'T work out.

Another common time signature is $\frac{3}{4}$ (or "three four"). Using the fraction analogy again, the quarter note still gets the beat (because there is a 4 on the bottom), but now there are only three beats per measure (because there is a 3 on top). That means each measure must contain the equivalent of three quarter notes. In $\frac{3}{4}$ time, the sum of the fractions each note represents should equal three fourths. Following are some examples of correct and incorrect measures in $\frac{3}{4}$ time:

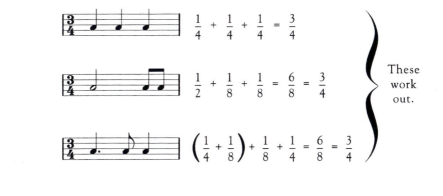

$$\frac{1}{4} + \frac{1}{4} + \frac{1}{4} = \frac{3}{4}$$

$$\frac{1}{2} + \frac{1}{8} + \frac{1}{8} = \frac{6}{8} = \frac{3}{4}$$

$$\left(\frac{1}{4} + \frac{1}{8}\right) + \frac{1}{8} + \frac{1}{4} = \frac{6}{8} = \frac{3}{4}$$

These work out.

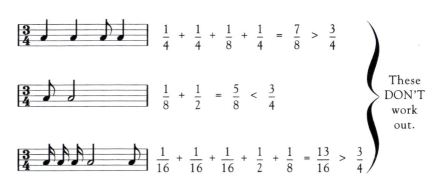

$$\frac{1}{4} + \frac{1}{4} + \frac{1}{8} + \frac{1}{4} = \frac{7}{8} > \frac{3}{4}$$

$$\frac{1}{8} + \frac{1}{2} = \frac{5}{8} < \frac{3}{4}$$

$$\frac{1}{16} + \frac{1}{16} + \frac{1}{16} + \frac{1}{2} + \frac{1}{8} = \frac{13}{16} > \frac{3}{4}$$

These DON'T work out.

Remember that the names for the notes are derived from $\frac{4}{4}$ time. Only in $\frac{4}{4}$ time does a quarter note actually take up one fourth of the measure. A quarter note in $\frac{3}{4}$ time takes up one third of a measure, but is still called a quarter note for consistency in notation.

Time signatures can be based on notes other than quarter notes. The bottom number indicates the note that equals one beat. Use the fraction analogy to determine that note when the bottom number is 2: dividing by 2 means multiplying by 1/2 so the note that gets the beat is a half note. In a time signature of $\frac{3}{2}$ there are three beats per measure, and the half note represents one beat. If there is an 8 on the bottom of a time signature, the note that gets the beat is an eighth note.

Here are some examples of measures that do and do not work. See if you can determine why in each case.

There is a many-leveled rhythm inherent in a piece of music. Pulses occur within each measure. For instance, in $\frac{4}{4}$ time the first and third beats are considered strong, and the second and fourth beats are considered weak. Music is said to be **syncopated** if the weak beats, or off-beats, are stressed, as is the case in big band music and jazz, in which tension is created by the sensation that notes don't fall where they are "supposed" to.

More subtle pulses occur by measure, creating distinctive rhythmic phrases. For example, the basic 12-bar blues phrase consists of 12 bars in $\frac{4}{4}$ time that naturally divide into three groups of four measures; there is an implied pulse on the first, fifth, and ninth measures, in addition to the natural pulses occurring within each measure and at the beginning of the complete 12-bar phrase.

Twelve-bar blues phrase

A line of melody has its very own rhythm—a phrase that flows above the more basic pulses grounded below it. The phrasing depends both on the type of music being played and, of course, on the preferred style of the musician, who adds his or her own expression to the rhythm. The Italian word *rubato* is used to imply, literally, the "robbing" of time. The musician can steal time by stretching out certain notes within a phrase, but must eventually give it back by speeding up others, so that the total time is the same as if the phrase were played straight.

No matter how complicated a musical rhythm gets, it can always be analyzed mathematically. One of the most difficult rhythmic tasks is playing one rhythm **against** another; that is, playing two different rhythmic cycles simultaneously in a given time period without compromising either one. For example, a piano piece might include a measure requiring the performer to play two notes of equal length with the right hand and three notes of equal length with the left hand.

This is called 2-against-3. One of the rhythmic cycles splits the given time period up into two equal parts, and one splits it into three equal parts. The problem is figuring out where the notes will fall in relation to one another. In $\frac{3}{4}$ time it's easy to see how to split the time period (one measure) into three equal parts:

But how can the measure simultaneously be split into two equal parts? The first note will fall on the first beat of the measure, along with the first note of the group of three notes, but the second note will necessarily fall between the remaining two notes:

The mathematical concept of the **least common multiple (LCM)** can be used to determine where the second note of two will fall in relation to the three-note rhythmic cycle. Since the LCM of 2 and 3 is 6, divide the measure into six equal parts (or counts) to determine where each note falls. The six-count measure could be counted "one *and* two *and* three *and*." (In a time signature of $\frac{3}{4}$, each of these counts represents an eighth note, since three quarter notes equal six eighth notes.)

In the measure below, the first rhythmic cycle has three quarter notes per measure, each taking up two counts. The first note is counted "one *and*," the second note is "two *and*," and the third note is "three *and*." The second rhythmic cycle has two dotted quarter notes per measure, each taking up three counts. The first dotted quarter note is counted "one *and* two." The second dotted quarter note begins on the *and* of two, and is counted "*and* three *and*."

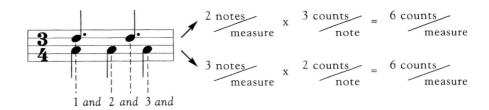

1 *and* 2 *and* 3 *and*

Assign one of these cycles to each of your hands and try to play them together, beating on a table or some other surface. It may help to count out loud to make sure that the beats are falling on the right count.

A more complicated rhythm is 3-against-4. The LCM of 3 and 4 is 12, so the measure is divided into 12 equal parts. (In this case, each part or count represents one sixteenth note, since three quarter notes equal twelve sixteenth notes.) This 12-count cycle can be counted "one *e and a*, two *e and a*, three *e and a*, four *e and a*."

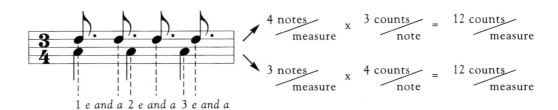

Try to beat out this rhythm as well. You may find that beating out a 2-against-3 rhythm is pretty easy, and that a 3-against-4 rhythm is possible to play, as well. But try 5-against-4 or 7-against-5 and you will see how quickly it gets very difficult, even with the aid of the LCM technique. Here are some examples from the music of Chopin.

22-against-12

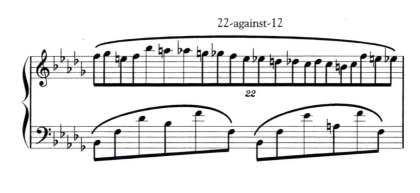

11-against-6

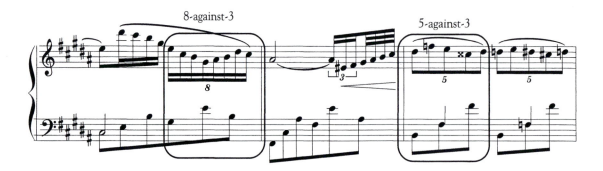

Indian music, in particular, has an incredibly complicated rhythmic structure. The player of the tabla, a pair of small hand drums, must master such complicated rhythms as 12-against-11 and 15-against-13. One hand divides a block of time into 15 equal parts while the other hand divides the same time period into 13 equal parts. This rhythmic pattern could be analyzed in the same way that the 2-against-3 and 3-against-4 rhythmic patterns were, but since the LCM of 15 and 13 is 195, the analysis certainly would not fit on this page!

The tabla player (shown on the following page) must have a gut feeling for what Mickey Hart calls "the One, the alpha and the omega, the beginning and the end of the rhythmic cycle."[2] The player, after countless hours of practice, simply knows when the two cycles (15 beats in one, 13 in the other) must come together again on "the One." In this case, mathematics can be used to analyze the rhythmic pattern, but isn't really much help in learning how to execute it.

The rhythmic complexity of African music is equally impressive. The belief exists in many parts of Africa that in order to lead a good life, one must entrain oneself with all external rhythms. It is not surprising, then, that the purpose of music is not the development of the melody, as it is in so much of the music we're used to in Western cultures, but the development of the rhythm.

A typical African musical ensemble consists of a large, low drum, up to 12 other drums, and a collection of iron bells, gongs, shawms (similar to oboes), and flutes. The music created by such an ensemble is **polyrhythmic**, meaning "having many rhythms." There are anywhere from two to six or seven rhythms going on at once. Although there is no dominant rhythm, one musician usually beats a short phrase on a gong or bell that is used as a mutual reference point by all the other musicians.

Anthropologists think that polyrhythmic music exists because of the belief that the presence of both a male and female principle is necessary to reach a state of perfection in any endeavor. In many parts of Africa, 3 is considered a male number, while 2 and 4 are considered female numbers. Therefore, having at least two different rhythms (one with a cycle of three beats, or some multiple of three; one with a cycle of two beats, or some multiple of two) fulfills the requirement of having both a male and female element.

Unlike Indian music, where the tabla player creates both rhythms, each drummer in an African ensemble has his own rhythm. A drum master from the Fanti tribe of Africa calls this the "hidden rhythm." The drummer practices this rhythm (usually a simple multiple of two or three) alone until he is good enough, and can keep time well enough, to attempt combining it with everyone else's. And he's not considered a true African drummer until he can keep his rhythm going while listening to two other rhythms at the same time. Mathematically speaking, the polyrhythm created by this ensemble is very complicated. Twos, threes, fours, sixes, and eights beat against each other creating a many-layered pulsating rhythm. The best dancers are those who express all the rhythms—a different one for each body part! Mathematics can be used to analyze the polyrhythms of African music, but the analysis turns out to be too complicated to be of practical use. The math still underlies the music, but there's no conscious effort on the part of the performer to use it.

The music of Bali and Java is also very percussive and rhythmically complicated. The typical ensemble is called a **gamelan**, and consists mostly of percussion, with maybe a few flutes and strings. There are two of each instrument—a male/female pair whose rhythms echo one another and overlap so subtly that it sounds like a single drum playing. The instruments reverberate with an intense, pulsing energy and weave a tapestry of rhythm that, like the polyrhythms of Africa, defies analysis.

Although different cultures and different eras have unique characteristic rhythms, rhythm is fundamental to all music. It sets the pulse and, therefore, the mood of the piece. A rhythm that beats 80 to 90 beats per minute is most similar to the body's natural rhythm, and will most likely create a sense of relaxation. Consider, on the other hand, the music Stravinsky wrote for Nijinsky's ballet *The Rite of Spring*, the story of a maiden who is chosen for the spring sacrifice and dances herself to death. The bizarre, violent rhythms, along with the strange, unconventional harmonies and choreography, caused an angry riot on opening night!

Music's rhythm can always be looked at through mathematical lenses. After all, how could one count out a rhythm in a Beethoven sonata or keep time in a jazz band without using numbers? Often, though, rhythm is felt more than analyzed, personalized rather than intellectualized, because music isn't an exact science as is mathematics. In the end, rhythm and the silent mathematics behind it allow the musician, listener, and dancer to entrain with the rhythms of nature and each other.

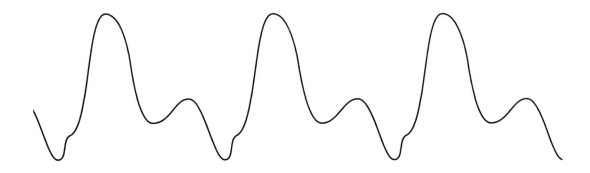

CHAPTER 3

THE TONE

EVERYTHING AROUND US is vibrating with a rhythm of its own. Protons and neutrons have rhythm, water moving in the ocean has a rhythm, the surface of the earth during an earthquake has a rhythm, the back-beat created by the drummer in a rock band has a rhythm. In each case, the source of the rhythm transfers the vibrations of the rhythm to the surrounding substance, or **medium**, whether it be air, water, the ground, or something else.

Whenever these vibrations disturb the medium in a regular, periodic way—that is, they repeat at equal time intervals—they create **wave motion**. The portion of a rhythm that is repeated over and over represents one **cycle** of the periodic motion, or one **wave**. A wave has a high point and a low point, just as a wave in the ocean has a **crest** and a **trough**.

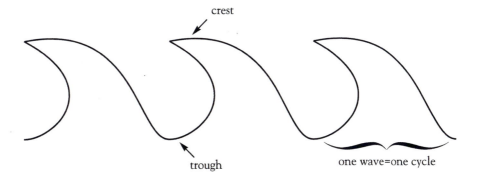

The first kind of wave we'll consider is called a **transverse wave**. In a transverse wave, the particles in the medium vibrate *perpendicular* to the direction in which the wave is traveling.

Transverse Wave

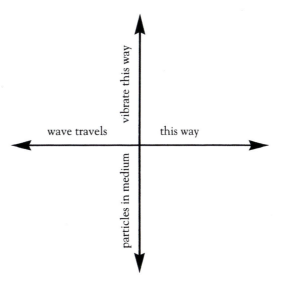

Imagine attaching a rope to a wall in front of you, standing away from the wall just enough to give the rope some slack, and then giving the rope a quick up-and-down jerk with your hand.

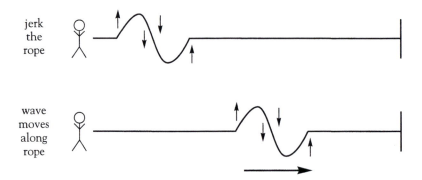

The movement of your hand sends a wave traveling horizontally along the rope, while the rope itself moves up and down, perpendicular to the direction of the wave's movement.

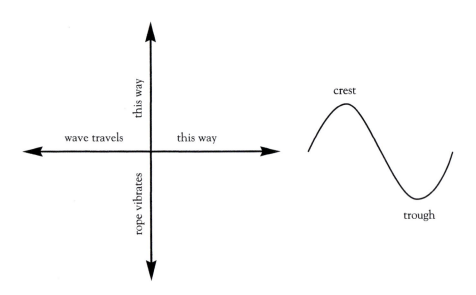

A violin string, when plucked, works just like the rope. The pluck, rather than the hand jerk, generates the wave. While the wave travels along the string horizontally, the string itself, and, therefore, the air particles around it, move ever-so-slightly in the vertical direction.

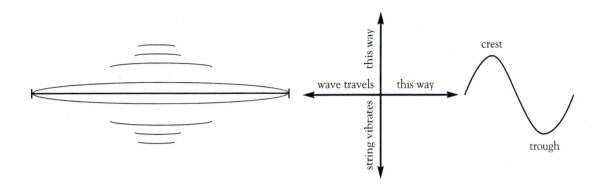

The transverse waves we're interested in are called **sine waves**.[3] Here are a couple of examples:

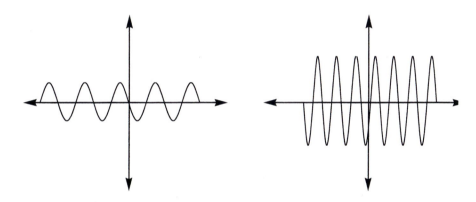

The other kind of wave to consider is called a **longitudinal wave**. In a longitudinal wave, the particles in the medium vibrate *parallel* to the direction in which the wave is travelling.

Longitudinal Waves

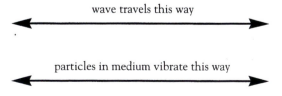

You send a longitudinal wave down a row of dominoes when you knock the first one over, because the dominoes fall in the direction of the wave.

Another example of a longitudinal wave is a Slinky® toy hung from the ceiling with a weight of some sort attached to the end. If you pull on the weight and then let go, the whole system bobs up and down. The wave (created by your pulling on the weight) and the medium (the Slinky) move parallel to one another.

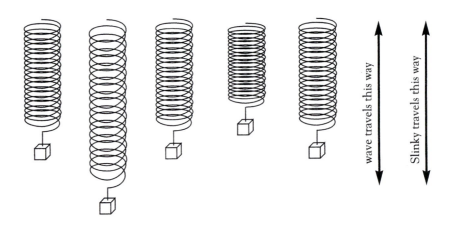

The Slinky will eventually stop bobbing and come to rest. But until then, the motion is periodic—a new wave starts traveling along the Slinky every time the weight reaches its lowest point. That means that as the wave travels along the Slinky, its coils will be close together at some places (called **points of compression**), and farther apart at others (called **points of rarefaction**).

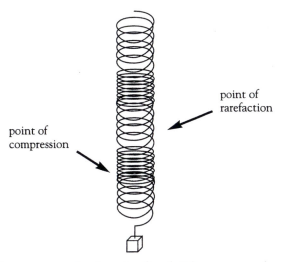

point of rarefaction

point of compression

Sound waves are also longitudinal. The source of a sound sends a vibration outward into the air. The vibration temporarily shoves the air particles away from their equilibrium (original) positions, each particle moving, on average, 1/100,000 inch.

At the points of compression, there are many air molecules crowded together and the pressure is high. At the points of rarefaction, the air molecules are more spread out and the pressure is low. The vibration, or **sound wave**, creates these compressions and rarefactions as it travels through the air.

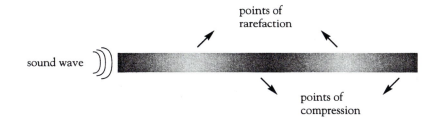

points of rarefaction

sound wave

points of compression

The wave that travels along a violin string when it is plucked is transverse, but the sound wave that the string transmits to the air is longitudinal. The longitudinal wave travels through the air, hits your eardrum, and allows you to hear the note.

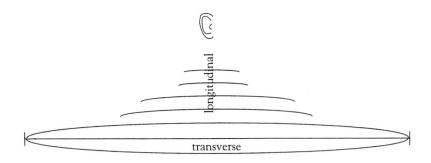

A direct correspondence can be drawn between the two kinds of waves: The crest of a transverse wave corresponds to a point of compression of a longitudinal wave, and a trough corresponds to a point of rarefaction.

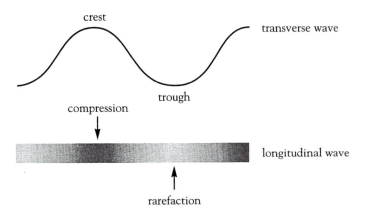

Sound waves, although longitudinal, are usually drawn as transverse waves. This is because it's easier to draw a sine wave than a multitude of tiny air molecules alternately compressed and spread out. In this book, all sound waves will be drawn as transverse waves. This visual representation is called a **waveform**.

All sound travels in waves. But not all sounds—and, therefore, not all sound waves—are the same. Compare the sounds made by the flute and the guitar, for instance. Their waveforms look quite different, because the flute has a mellow sound and the guitar has a sharper sound.

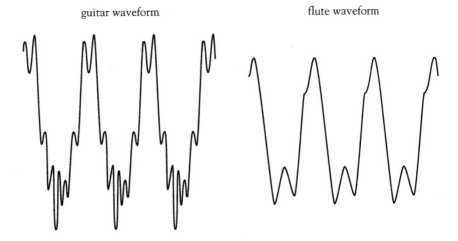

guitar waveform   flute waveform

What makes one sound wave different from another, and, therefore, some sounds more musical than others? Although the decision about what is music and what is noise is really a personal, subjective one, music is generally distinguished from noise by the regularity of the sound waves that create musical sounds. The regularity of a wave is determined by certain characteristic quantities called **amplitude**, **frequency**, and **wavelength**.

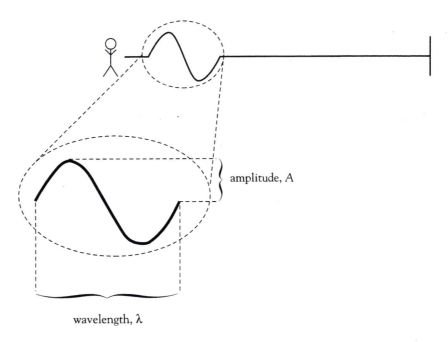

amplitude, A

wavelength, λ

Remember the example of the rope on page 22. The distance from the top of the crest of the wave to the **equilibrium** (original) position of the rope, or from the bottom of the trough of the wave to the equilibrium position (the distance is the same in both cases), is called the **amplitude (A)** of the wave. The amplitude, then, is the maximum displacement from the equilibrium position.

The **wavelength** (λ) is the distance between any point on one wave and the corresponding point on the next one; that is, the distance the wave travels in one cycle.

The **frequency** (*f*) is the number of waves, or vibrations, that pass a given point per second. The frequency of the wave is the same as the frequency of the source. Frequency is measured in **Hertz (Hz)**, where 1 Hz = 1 vibration/second, after Heinrich Rudolf Hertz, a German physicist who lived during the 1800s.[4]

The **period (T)** is the time it takes for one whole wave or cycle to pass a given point. Therefore, the period (number of seconds per wave) and the frequency (number of waves per second) are reciprocals of one another, and $T = 1/f$.

These quantities—amplitude, frequency, wavelength, and period—are all measurable physical characteristics of any musical tone.

The **loudness** of a tone is the listener's evaluation of the amplitude—the larger the amplitude, the louder the tone; the smaller the amplitude, the softer the tone. Loudness is measured in **decibels**.[5]

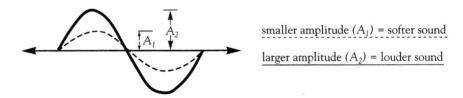

smaller amplitude (A_1) = softer sound

larger amplitude (A_2) = louder sound

The **pitch** of a tone is the listener's evaluation of the frequency, and represents how high or low a note sounds. The higher the frequency (the more vibrations per second), the higher the pitch; the lower the frequency (the fewer vibrations per second), the lower the pitch.

A musical **tone** lasts long enough and is steady enough to have pitch, quality (timbre), and loudness. A drum usually makes a short, sharp sound that encompasses many different frequencies, never settling in on one. Consequently, the sound disappears quickly and doesn't have a discernible pitch; therefore, it is not a tone.

A **pure** or **simple tone** has constant frequency and amplitude and has the shape of a sine curve.

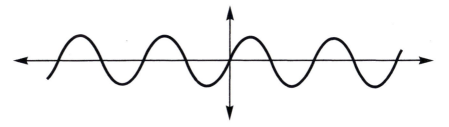

What happens when two or more pure tones are combined? What does the new, or **resultant**, waveform look like? It turns out that the resultant waveform can be discerned by adding the two original waveforms' displacements from equilibrium at each point. The following diagram shows the addition of two waveforms that have the same frequency but different amplitudes:

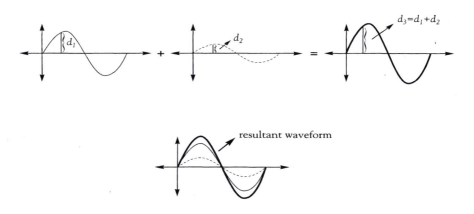

In this example, the crests of the two original waves occur at the same time, as do the troughs. The waves are said to be **in phase**. If the crest of one wave occurs at the same point as the trough of the other, the waves are **in opposite phase**.

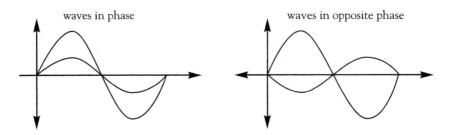

waves in phase   waves in opposite phase

Waves that are in opposite phase are added in the same way as are waves that are in phase. (Note that displacement below the horizontal axis is negative.)

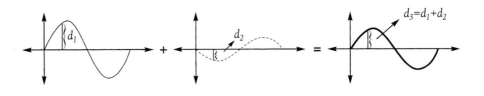

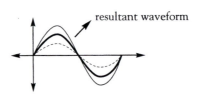

resultant waveform

When combining tones, it is most common for waves to be **out of phase**; that is, for there to be no particular relationship between the position of the crests and troughs. Again, the resultant waveform can be found by adding displacements.

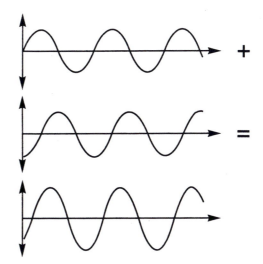

In the preceding diagram, the two original waves had the same frequency. Waveforms with different frequencies can also be added.

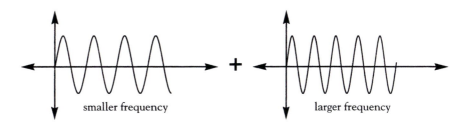

smaller frequency   larger frequency

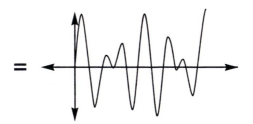

Consider the case of two pure tones with exactly the same amplitude and frequency played in opposite phase. Using addition of displacements to find the resultant waveform, it appears as if the two originals completely cancel each other out and no sound is heard whatsoever.

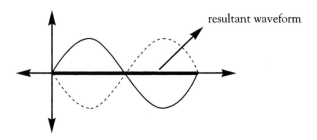

resultant waveform

Why, then, when listening to music, don't we hear occasional empty spots where the sound just disappears because the sound waves are in opposite phase? Part of the reason is that a truly pure tone with constant frequency and amplitude is impossible to create without the use of electronic instruments. Most musical tones are **complex**, meaning they're formed by adding a number of component waves. These components are called **partials**, and each has a different pure-tone frequency. The number, frequencies, and amplitudes of the individual partials describe the quality of the complex tone. The number of partials produced on a vibrating string depends on where the string is plucked, and how hard it is plucked (for example, soft tones are composed of fewer partials than loud tones).

In a complex tone, the partial with the smallest pure-tone frequency is called the **fundamental**, and its frequency is called the **fundamental frequency** (f). In most musical tones, the frequencies of the partials are integer multiples ($2f$, $3f$, $4f$, . . .) of the fundamental frequency. Such a tone is said to be made from its **harmonics** or **harmonic overtones**. (If the frequencies of the partials are not integer multiples of the fundamental frequency, an **inharmonic tone** is produced.) The first partial, with fundamental frequency f, is the first harmonic; the second partial, with frequency $2f$, is the second harmonic; and so on.[6]

For instance, if the fundamental frequency of a tone is 100 Hz (vibrations per second), these are the frequencies of the first four harmonics:

1st harmonic	f	=	100 Hz
2nd harmonic	$2f$	=	200 Hz
3rd harmonic	$3f$	=	300 Hz
4th harmonic	$4f$	=	400 Hz

If the fundamental frequency is 220 Hz, these are the frequencies:

1st harmonic	f	=	220 Hz
2nd harmonic	$2f$	=	440 Hz
3rd harmonic	$3f$	=	660 Hz
4th harmonic	$4f$	=	880 Hz

Since a complex tone produced on a vibrating string is made up of its harmonics, it's almost as if the string has a polyrhythm of its own—the individual harmonics are the individual rhythms that come together on "the One." They "beat" together because the frequencies of the harmonics are integer multiples of the fundamental frequency.

Noise is technically created by a mixture of many different partials with many different frequencies. **White noise**—analogous to white light—is a special kind of noise that contains equal amounts of sound power from each portion of the spectrum of available frequencies. It sounds a lot like air escaping from a hole in a tire.

What happens when two tones with slightly different frequencies are heard together? The sound waves interfere with each other, sometimes combining to make a louder sound, and sometimes partially or fully cancelling each other out to make a softer sound. This pulsing pattern of louds and softs is called **beats**.

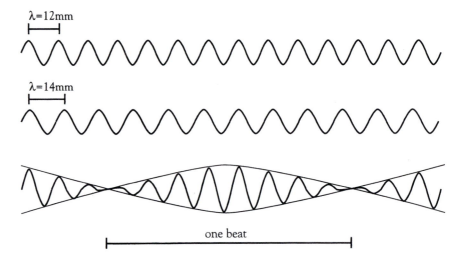

The number of beats or pulses heard per second is called the **beat frequency**, and is simply the difference between the frequencies of the two original tones. For example, if a piano tuner is tuning a piano with a 440 Hz tuning fork and the string produces a tone with frequency 445 Hz, the beat frequency is 445 Hz − 440 Hz = 5 Hz; he or she hears fifteen beats per second.

If the beat frequency produced by two tones with different frequencies is rapid enough, a **difference tone** is heard. Difference tones are quite soft, and are always lower than the higher of the two original tones, so the ear usually ignores them. But on the flute, with its high frequencies, they are often heard distinctly as third notes, giving the impression that two flautists are somehow playing a trio! For example, two tones with frequencies 1,244 Hz and 1,046 Hz would produce a difference tone with frequency 1,244 Hz − 1,046 Hz = 198 Hz. Sometimes, difference tones conflict with other notes already being played, and can be quite annoying.

Two tones in **unison** (same frequency) blend together and produce no beats. If the pitch of one of the tones is increased, the number of beats heard per second also increases, creating a discord that makes the tones sound out of tune. The tones are most discordant, or **dissonant**, when the beat frequency is about 25 or 30 Hz—beyond that, the unpleasantness decreases and finally disappears.

Whether or not groups of notes sound discordant or dissonant is a measure of whether or not they are in tune relative to one another. This brings up the question of whether or not there is truly an objective "in tune." The standard set around the world today is the tone, called **A**, produced by a frequency of 440 Hz. Orchestras, piano tuners, and makers of electronic instruments use this standard as a basis for tuning.

It hasn't always been this way. Handel (1685–1759) used a tuning fork for A with a frequency of 422.5 Hz. However, since stringed instruments seem to sound more brilliant when tuned to higher frequencies, the frequency of A kept inching up. By the 1800s, it had reached 455 Hz in Great Britain and 461 Hz in the United States. The frequency probably would have kept rising, had not the standard of 440 Hz been agreed to in 1953. Most orchestras now use a frequency of 440 Hz for the A that all the instruments tune to, but some still tune to 442 or 444 Hz.

It seems, then, that there is no objective "in tune"—a Platonic Form, so to speak, representing the way in which music is meant to be produced. The important thing is that vibrations of the individual waves are in harmony with one another. Their rhythms are so rapid that we are rarely aware of the individual beats, but we certainly are aware of the music created when they blend in just the right way.

CHAPTER 4

THE TUNE

FOR MANY CENTURIES, mathematics and music have been perceived as related disciplines. Mathematics is the study of number, pattern, and form, and these elements are inherent in the science, composition, and performance of music. But although the connection between mathematics and music has been evident since ancient times, the character of this connection has changed quite dramatically over the years.

Mathematics was born out of practical necessity and consisted, in the beginning, simply of numbers and counting. Ancient peoples needed to keep track of their herds and crops, and to conduct business at the market. So they developed gestures and words for numbers. In many cultures, the words came directly from the finger and hand positions of the counting gestures. Some languages had very unspecific number systems with words only for one, two, a few, several, and many. In fact, the Indo-European root words for the first three numbers are *oi* (meaning "this here"), *du* (meaning "that there"), and *ter* (meaning "that, beyond").

We'll probably never know how much influence the development of a number system had on the music of a given culture, or vice versa. It's likely that primitive people had a sense of rhythm and the grouping of musical beats long before number words existed to count out the rhythms. At some point, however, the developing counting and grouping systems probably began to affect the music.

Early on the interplay between math and music was subtle and most likely more felt than thought out. By the time of the ancient Greeks, music was defined and even restricted by the mathematics that dictated its theory. The relationship between the two disciplines has gone through many changes since then. Now, although mathematics still provides a basis for music theory, music is not thought of as a strictly mathematical discipline. The historical development of tuning theory, which involves the mathematical relationships that dictate the tuning of an instrument, sheds much light on the nature of this transition. For practical purposes, our discussion of this theory will center on the piano.

The piano keyboard consists of 88 white and black keys and a pattern that repeats every 12 keys. The portion that repeats contains 7 white keys and 5 black keys.

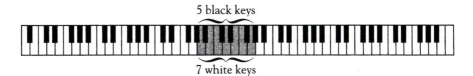

The white keys are given the letter names A through G, and the black keys are denoted by a letter name followed by a sharp symbol (♯) or a flat symbol (♭), depending on the situation. For instance, the black key between C and D has two names: C♯ and D♭.

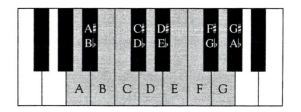

The distance between two adjacent keys on the piano is called a **half step** (for example, between C and C♯, or E and F); two half steps make a **whole step** (for example, between C and D, or E and F♯). A sharp raises a note a half step, while a flat lowers it a half step.

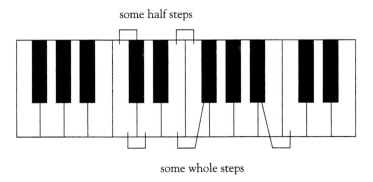

some half steps

some whole steps

A **scale** is a series of musical tones with specified distances, or **intervals,** between them. If you start with any C on a piano keyboard and play all the white notes up to the next C (call it C*), you will hear the familiar **major scale** on which so much of Western music is based. The major scale is made up of two whole steps, a half step, three more whole steps, and another half step. The syllables *do*, *re*, *mi*, *fa*, *sol*, *la*, and *ti* are often used to name the seven tones of the major scale.

C-major scale

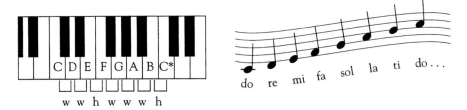

w w h w w w h

do re mi fa sol la ti do . . .

This scale can be played in any **key;** that is, if you start on any note and proceed to play the correct succession of half and whole steps, you'll be playing a major scale in the key of whatever note was first. For example, to play a major scale in the key of A, called an A-major scale, begin on A and proceed as follows:

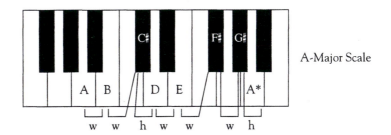

A-Major Scale

When you play the sequence of notes in the A-major scale, the pitches seem to resolve at the end. A* sounds like the natural conclusion to this particular group of notes. That's because A and A* sound alike, except that A* is higher. A and A* form an interval called an **octave** because A* is the eighth note in the scale. In fact, all the As on the keyboard sound similar except some are higher in pitch while others are lower. Call the lowest key on the piano A. Going up the keyboard, A_1 is an octave above A, A_2 is two octaves above A, A_5 is three octaves above A_2, and so on. The keyboard runs from A to C_8 and spans a little more than seven octaves. C_4 is called **middle C** because it's near the middle of the keyboard, and is often used as a reference point.

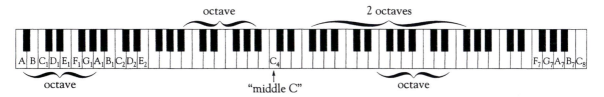

Notice that not all adjacent notes in a major scale are the same distance apart. Since a whole step consists of two half steps, the whole steps sound farther apart. If you start with A_3 and play all the keys, white and black, up to A_4, you will hear what's called the **chromatic scale.** In this scale of 13 notes, all adjacent notes sound the same distance apart; that is, the octave is divided into 12 evenly spaced half steps.

The frequencies, in Hertz (vibrations per second), of the notes in this scale produced by a piano are the following (rounded to the nearest tenth):

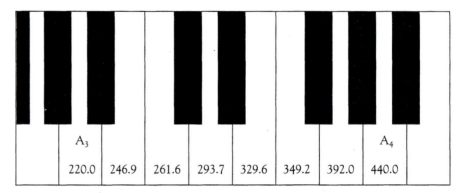

A₃							A₄
220.0	246.9	261.6	293.7	329.6	349.2	392.0	440.0

Notice that the frequency of A_4 (440 Hz) is exactly twice that of A_3 (220 Hz). This is no mere coincidence. For any two notes that are an octave apart, the ratio of the frequency of the high note to the frequency of the low note is always $2:1$.

Consider the harmonics (the sound waves that create a complex tone—see pages 32–33) of these two tones:

A_3		A_4	
$1f$	220 Hz	$1f$	440 Hz
$2f$	440 Hz	$2f$	880 Hz
$3f$	660 Hz	$3f$	1320 Hz
$4f$	880 Hz		
$5f$	1100 Hz		
$6f$	1320 Hz		

The harmonics of A_4 have the same frequencies as every other harmonic of A_3. That is, the ear hears parts of A_3 when A_4 is played, creating the sensation that the two tones are somehow alike.

The frequencies of the tones in an octave have a very obvious relationship, $2:1$. In addition, a special relationship exists between any two adjacent notes in the chromatic scale. Since all half steps in the chromatic scale sound the same distance apart, the frequencies of all the pitches should be somehow related. Close inspection reveals that the frequency of any note is the product of the frequency of the note before it and a constant factor. Simple arithmetic shows that factor to be 1.059463094 . . . . That is, the frequencies of any two adjacent notes are in the ratio 1.059 . . . : 1. For example:

$$\frac{\text{freq. of A}\sharp_3}{\text{freq. of A}_3} = \frac{233.1 \text{ Hz}}{220 \text{ Hz}} \approx 1.059\ldots \qquad \frac{\text{eq. of G}_4}{\text{eq. of F}\sharp_4} = \frac{392.0 \text{ Hz}}{370.0 \text{ Hz}} \approx 1.059\ldots$$

$$\frac{\text{freq. of C}_4}{\text{freq. of B}_3} = \frac{261.6 \text{ Hz}}{246.9 \text{ Hz}} \approx 1.059\ldots \qquad \begin{aligned} \text{freq. of A}_4 &= \text{freq. of A}\flat_4 \times 1.059\ldots \\ &= 415.3 \text{ Hz} \times 1.059\ldots \\ &= 440 \text{ Hz} \end{aligned}$$

A graph of the situation is an exponential curve:

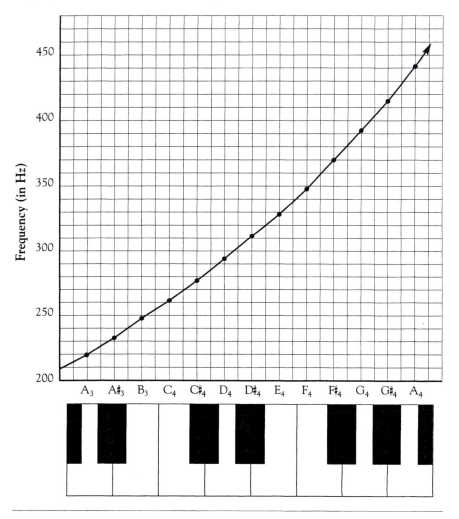

Where does the number 1.059 . . . come from? There are 12 half steps in an octave. A and A$\sharp$, for example, form an interval of a half step. Call the ratio of their frequencies h. Then, $\frac{A\sharp}{A} = h$ and A$\sharp$ = A $\cdot$ h. The following pattern emerges:

$$A\sharp = A \cdot h$$
$$B = A\sharp \cdot h = (A \cdot h)\, h = A \cdot h^2$$
$$C = B \cdot h = (A \cdot h^2)\, h = A \cdot h^3$$
$$\vdots$$

$$A* = A \cdot h^{12}$$

This implies that $\dfrac{A*}{A} = h^{12}$ and $h = \sqrt[12]{\dfrac{A*}{A}}$

But since A and A* form an octave, $\dfrac{A*}{A} = \dfrac{2}{1}$, and

$$h = \sqrt[12]{2} \approx 1.059463094 \ldots$$

So to find the frequencies of the notes between A_3 and A_4, you would proceed as follows:

A_3
$$220 \cdot \sqrt[12]{2} \cdot \sqrt[12]{2} \cdot \sqrt[12]{2} \cdot \sqrt[12]{2} \cdot \sqrt[12]{2} \cdot \sqrt[12]{2} \cdot \sqrt[12]{2} \cdot \sqrt[12]{2} \cdot \sqrt[12]{2} \cdot \sqrt[12]{2} \cdot \sqrt[12]{2} \cdot \sqrt[12]{2}$$

| $A\sharp_3 \to$ 233.1 |
| $B_3 \to$ 246.9 |
| $C_4 \to$ 261.6 |
| $C\sharp_4 \to$ 277.2 |
| $D_4 \to$ 293.7 |
| $D\sharp_4 \to$ 311.1 |
| $E_4 \to$ 329.6 |
| $F_4 \to$ 349.2 |
| $F\sharp_4 \to$ 370.0 |
| $G_4 \to$ 392.0 |
| $G\sharp_4 \to$ 415.3 |
| $A_4 \to$ 440.0 |

Within any octave, the frequency relationships are as follows:

Do		Re		Mi	Fa		Sol		La		Ti	Do
f	$2^{\frac{1}{12}}f$	$2^{\frac{1}{6}}f$	$2^{\frac{1}{4}}f$	$2^{\frac{1}{3}}f$	$2^{\frac{5}{12}}f$	$2^{\frac{1}{2}}f$	$2^{\frac{7}{12}}f$	$2^{\frac{2}{3}}f$	$2^{\frac{3}{4}}f$	$2^{\frac{5}{6}}f$	$2^{\frac{11}{12}}f$	$2f$

The frequencies of the rest of the notes on the piano can be found by successively multiplying and dividing by h.

When an instrument is tuned to these frequencies, with the octave divided into 12 equal parts and the frequency ratio between half steps equal to 1.059 . . . , it is said to be **even-tempered,** or tuned in **equal temperament.**

Equal temperament provides only one of many possible ways of assigning intervals to a scale. What is the advantage of dividing the octave into only 12 tones? After all, the audible range of frequencies is approximately from 20 Hz to 20,000 Hz, and there are an infinite number of frequencies, and therefore tones, within this range, and also an infinite number of frequencies within an octave. Practically speaking, a trained musical ear can only distinguish about 100 different tones within an octave—not an infinite number. The actual number of tones used in musical composition and performance is much smaller; a simple melody consists of only a few notes, a piano keyboard has only 88 keys, and even a full symphony orchestra can produce only a finite number of audible pitches.

The number of notes in a scale varies from culture to culture. Twenty-four-hundred-year-old sets of musical bells based on a 12-tone scale have been unearthed in China. And in Asian music, the octave is usually divided into 24 or so tones—within each interval of a half step there are two **quarter tones.** However, most cultures around the world divide the huge spectrum of tones in an octave into scales consisting of 5 to 7 notes.

The system of intervals from which a scale is composed also varies from culture to culture. For example, most African music divides the octave into 7 notes (8, including the octave), as does Western music. But some of the frequency intervals between notes in African music may seem too long or too short to an ear trained in the Western tradition. That is, some notes sound too high, or sharp, and some notes sound too low, or flat, and therefore out of tune. Western music probably sounds just as out of tune to an African.

The unique harmonies of the blues and jazz were born out of this difference in intervals. When African slaves sang Christian songs, they flattened slightly the third and seventh notes of the scale. And African-American jazz musicians used notes that couldn't actually be played on the piano—because they seemed to slip between the keys into the cracks—called **blue notes.** When we write down the music of other cultures in terms of familiar Western scales, we are to a certain extent approximating and distorting.

In fact, we are also only approximating when we write down and play the music of other time periods in terms of currently used scales. Since our instruments are tuned in equal temperament, our scales have intervals created by those frequencies. But equal temperament is a relatively recent innovation; instruments have not always been tuned in a way that divides the octave into 12 equal parts. Part of the reason is that this division relies on the use of the irrational number $\sqrt[12]{2}$ (or $2^{1/12}$). The existence of irrational numbers was actually proved by the Greeks some time near the end of the fifth century B.C.[7] However, people had difficulty grasping the concept of a number that can't be expressed as a fraction and whose decimal portion neither repeats nor terminates. Students in math classes today are still overwhelmed when first introduced to numbers that they can't actually finish writing down.

$$\pi = 3.141592654\ldots$$
$$\sqrt{2} = 1.414213562\ldots$$

So instead of redefining the concept of number to include irrationals, the Greeks simply ignored them. Integers and rational numbers that can be expressed as ratios of integers were much preferred to the ghostly irrational numbers.

The technical definition of a *tuning* for an instrument is "a method for creating intervals that can be expressed in integer ratio," whereas *temperament* is "a modification of tuning that uses irrational numbers to express the ratios of some or all of its intervals." Before the advent of equal temperament, the methods for tuning instruments were truly tunings in the strict sense—the intervals were defined by ratios of integers.

The science of music, as it relates to finding mathematical relationships that dictate the tuning of an instrument, began with the discovery that the pitch of the tone produced by a vibrating string depends on the length of the string. This is the basic principle upon which the construction of stringed instruments is based.

There is reason to believe that this discovery was made as long ago as 3000 B.C. Stringed and wind instruments have been found in Babylon, Sumer, and ancient Egypt with string lengths and the spacing of finger holes based on mathematical proportions.

Ancient people also understood the concept that a ratio between two numbers is an entity. This concept is essential in music theory, since a ratio can represent the relationship between two tones (for example, C♯:C = 1.059 . . ., in equal temperament).

The first influential figure on the Western musical scene to consider is Pythagoras, the renowned Greek mathematician. He and his followers, the Pythagoreans, had many mystical beliefs about whole numbers and their relationship to the order of the universe:

> God has ordered the universe by means of numbers. God is unity, the world is plurality, and it consists of contrasting elements. It is harmony which restores unity to the contrasting parts and which moulds them into a cosmos. Harmony is divine, it consists of numerical ratios. Whosoever acquires full understanding of this number harmony, he becomes himself divine and immortal.[8]

The Pythagoreans believed that all regularities in nature were musical, and that the study of numbers and their relationship to musical harmony was the way to reach divine spiritual understanding and purity of soul. This was the beginning of an entirely mathematically based music theory.

There is reason to believe that Pythagoras traveled to Mesopotamia and learned and brought back many important mathematical ideas. Some of his findings may have inspired his experiments with the **monochord.** A monochord is a very simple instrument consisting of a string stretched taut over a moveable bridge. When the string is plucked, it vibrates and produces a tone. The pitch of the tone changes as the bridge is moved. Therefore, the pitch must be somehow related to the length of the portion of the string that's vibrating.

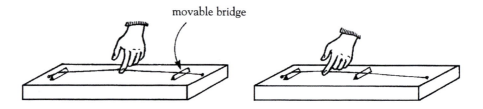
movable bridge

Pythagoras noticed that the pitch that resulted from shortening the string to exactly half its original length sounded similar to the original pitch, except it was higher—an octave higher, to be exact. The ratio of the new length (higher pitch) to the original length (lower pitch) is $(1/2):1$, or $1:2$.

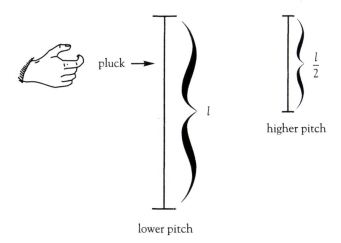

pluck →

l

lower pitch

$\dfrac{l}{2}$

higher pitch

As discussed earlier in this chapter, in an octave, the ratio of the new frequency (higher pitch) to the old frequency (lower pitch) is $2:1$. Notice, therefore, that the frequency ratio and the string length ratio are *reciprocals* of one another.

$$\text{frequency ratio} = \frac{f_{\text{new}}}{f_{\text{old}}} = \frac{2}{1}$$

$$\text{string-length ratio} = \frac{l_{\text{new}}}{l_{\text{old}}} = \frac{\frac{1}{2}}{1} = \frac{1}{2}$$

reciprocals

For example, consider a monochord with a string that is 20 centimeters long. Suppose the tone that sounds when the whole string is plucked has a frequency of 300 Hz. Now, move the bridge to shorten the string to half its length, 10 centimeters. The tone that sounds when half the string is plucked is an octave higher. Since the string lengths are in the ratio $1:2$ (half : whole), the ratio of frequencies of the higher tone (half of the string) to the lower tone (the whole string) must be in the ratio $2:1$. The higher tone, then, has frequency 600 Hz, since $600:300 = 2:1$.

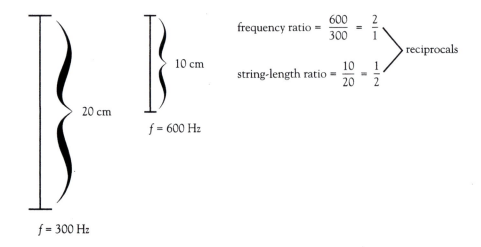

$$\text{frequency ratio} = \frac{600}{300} = \frac{2}{1}$$

$$\text{string-length ratio} = \frac{10}{20} = \frac{1}{2}$$

reciprocals

10 cm

$f = 600$ Hz

20 cm

$f = 300$ Hz

The audible "distance" between the pitch of the new tone (produced by part of the string) and the pitch of the original tone (produced by the whole string) changes as the bridge is moved. That is, the interval, represented by the frequency ratio, changes.

Now, suppose you have two monochords, with strings the same length. Imagine the sounds you would produce if you plucked both strings at the same time, leaving the bridge in place on one monochord while moving the bridge around on the other. Sometimes, the interval created by the different pitches sounds "good," and sometimes it doesn't. Intervals that sound good are called **consonant**—literally, they "sound together," or agree. Intervals that don't sound good are called **dissonant.**

In his experiments, Pythagoras found three intervals he considered to be consonant—the *diapason*, the *diapente*, and the *diatesaron*. We call these intervals the **octave,** the **fifth,** and the **fourth** because they correspond to the eighth, fifth, and fourth notes of what is known as the Pythagorean diatonic scale (which, as will be shown, is almost the same as the major scale discussed previously).

While the octave is obtained by shortening the string to one half its original length, the fifth is the interval that results from shortening the string to two thirds of its original length. Remember, it's called the fifth because it corresponds to the fifth note of the scale. For example, if you start with a monochord whose string, when plucked, produces the first note of a scale (*do*), two-thirds of the string, when plucked, will yield the fifth note of that scale (*sol*). The ratio of the new length to the original length in this case is $(2/3):1$, or $2:3$. The ratio of frequencies is the reciprocal, $3:2$. So if the original tone has frequency $300\,\text{Hz}$, the new frequency is $450\,\text{Hz}$, since $450:300 = 3:2$.

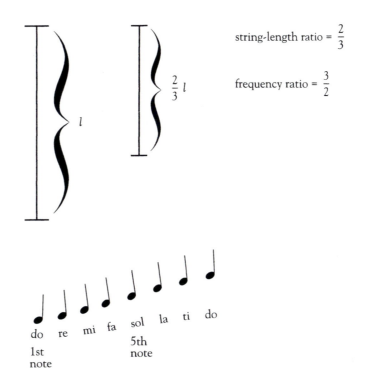

The final consonant interval is called the fourth, because it corresponds to the fourth note of the scale. It is produced when the string is shortened to three fourths of its original length. For example, shortening the given string to 3/4 its length yields *fa*, the fourth note of the scale. The ratio of string lengths here is $(3/4):1$, or $3:4$, while the ratio of frequencies is $4:3$. The new tone, then, must have frequency 400, since $400:300 = 4:3$.

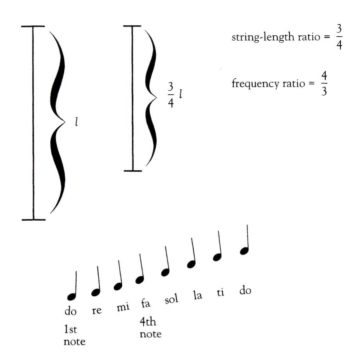

$$\text{string-length ratio} = \frac{3}{4}$$

$$\text{frequency ratio} = \frac{4}{3}$$

do re mi fa sol la ti do

do
1st
note

fa
4th
note

The Pythagoreans had no understanding of sound waves and frequency, nor of how the anatomy of the ear affects the pitch of a tone. In fact, the rule stating that frequency is related to string length wasn't even formulated until the seventeenth century, when the Franciscan Friar Marin Mersenne defined some rules about the frequency of a vibrating string.[9] Nonetheless, the Pythagoreans could still appreciate the beauty inherent in the discovery that ratios of whole numbers produced consonant intervals. The numbers in these ratios, namely, 1, 2, 3, and 4, add up to 10, the Pythagorean holy number. These numbers also made up what the Pythagoreans called the *holy tetractys*—a triangle with four rows representing the dimensions of experience.

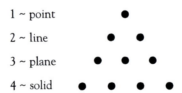

1 ~ point

2 ~ line

3 ~ plane

4 ~ solid

And from the idea that small number ratios could harmonize came the theory of means, which defines the arithmetic, geometric, and harmonic means.[10]

Pythagoras' experiments with the monochord led to a method for tuning instruments with intervals in integer ratio, known as **Pythagorean tuning.** The scale produced by this tuning, called the **Pythagorean diatonic scale,** was used for many years in the Western world. It can be derived from the monochord, and, consistent with Pythagorean doctrine, all of its intervals can be expressed as ratios of integers.

Let's build a diatonic scale based on a monochord whose string, when plucked, produces C_1. Three fourths of the string, when plucked, yields the fourth (fourth note) F_1; two thirds of the string yields the fifth (fifth note) G_1; and one half of the string yields the octave (eighth note) called C_2. Remember that the frequency ratio is the reciprocal of the string-length ratio.

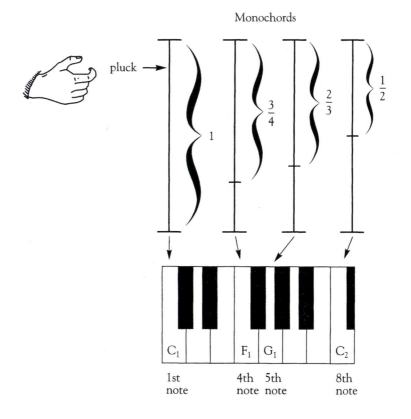

Monochords

It is now possible to find the remaining notes of the scale. For instance, to find D_1 on the monochord, first move a fifth up to G_1 by moving the bridge to two thirds of the length of the string. Then move up another fifth to D_2 by finding two thirds of the new length. Finally, move down an octave to D_1 by doubling the string's length.

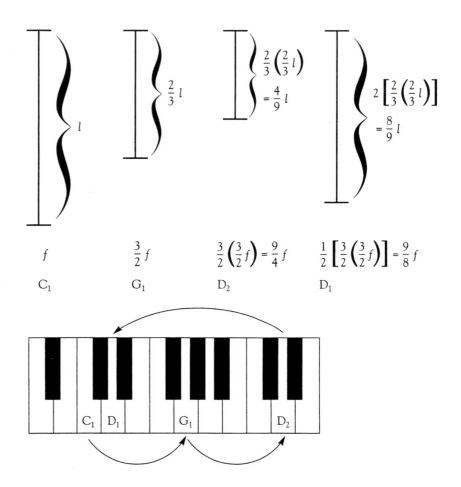

$$f \qquad \frac{3}{2}f \qquad \frac{3}{2}\left(\frac{3}{2}f\right)=\frac{9}{4}f \qquad \frac{1}{2}\left[\frac{3}{2}\left(\frac{3}{2}f\right)\right]=\frac{9}{8}f$$

$$C_1 \qquad\qquad G_1 \qquad\qquad D_2 \qquad\qquad D_1$$

The string length ratio is $8:9$; that is, a string that produces D_1 will be eight ninths as long as a string that produces C_1. Therefore, the frequency ratio should be the reciprocal, $9:8$. To get this ratio mathematically, combine the individual frequency ratios. When you move up a given interval, multiply by the frequency ratio of that interval; when you move down a given interval, divide by the frequency ratio of that interval.

You can find the rest of the notes in the scale the same way you found D_1. The general rule is to go up by fifths (by shortening the string) until you reach the note you're after, and then jump down by octaves (by lengthening the string) until you reach that note in the position you want. To find A_1, for instance, move up three fifths, from C_1 to G_1, from G_1 to D_2, and from D_2 to A_2, and then down an octave to A_1.

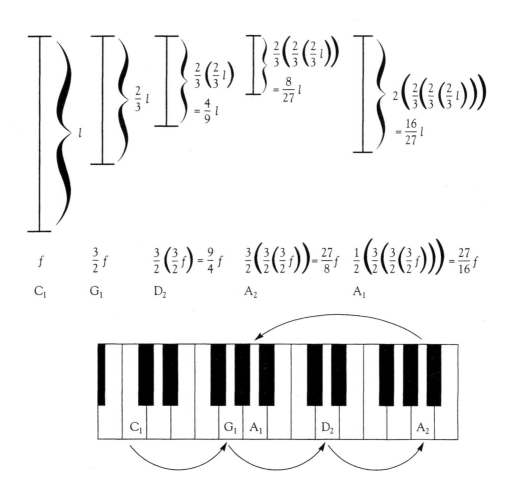

$$f \qquad \frac{3}{2}f \qquad \frac{3}{2}\left(\frac{3}{2}f\right)=\frac{9}{4}f \qquad \frac{3}{2}\left(\frac{3}{2}\left(\frac{3}{2}f\right)\right)=\frac{27}{8}f \qquad \frac{1}{2}\left(\frac{3}{2}\left(\frac{3}{2}\left(\frac{3}{2}f\right)\right)\right)=\frac{27}{16}f$$

$$C_1 \qquad\qquad G_1 \qquad\qquad D_2 \qquad\qquad\qquad A_2 \qquad\qquad\qquad\qquad A_1$$

To find E_1, move up four fifths, then down two octaves; to find B_1, move up five fifths, then down two octaves.

To find E_1: $\left(\dfrac{2}{3}\right)^4 \left(\dfrac{2}{1}\right)^2 l = \dfrac{64}{81} l$

$\left(\dfrac{3}{2}\right)^4 \left(\dfrac{1}{2}\right)^2 f = \dfrac{81}{64} f$

up   down
four   two
fifths   octaves

To find B_1: $\left(\dfrac{2}{3}\right)^5 \left(\dfrac{2}{1}\right)^2 l = \dfrac{128}{243} l$

$\left(\dfrac{3}{2}\right)^5 \left(\dfrac{1}{2}\right)^2 f = \dfrac{243}{128} f$

up   down
five   two
fifths   octaves

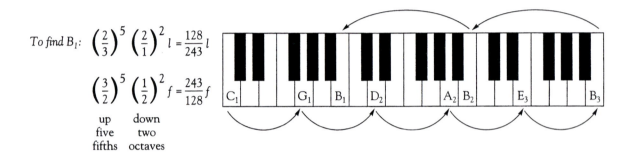

Now the scale is complete:

				fourth	fifth		octave
Note	C_1	D_1	E_1	F_1	G_1	A_1	B_1	C_2
string length	l	$\dfrac{8}{9} l$	$\dfrac{64}{81} l$	$\dfrac{3}{4} l$	$\dfrac{2}{3} l$	$\dfrac{16}{27} l$	$\dfrac{128}{243} l$	$\dfrac{1}{2} l$
frequency	f	$\dfrac{9}{8} f$	$\dfrac{81}{64} f$	$\dfrac{4}{3} f$	$\dfrac{3}{2} f$	$\dfrac{27}{16} f$	$\dfrac{243}{128} f$	$2f$

The ratio between the fifth and the fourth was defined by the Greeks as the **whole tone.** It is obtained by finding the difference between the frequencies of the fourth and the fifth intervals. Therefore, a whole tone in the diatonic scale has a frequency ratio of $9:8$, because $(3/2)/(4/3) = 9/8$. Note that the frequency ratio between F_1 and E_1 and between C_2 and B_1 is $256:243$ because $(4/3)/(81/64) = 256/243$ and $2/(243/128) = 256/243$. These intervals are called **semitones.**

The diatonic scale, then, consists of a sequence of whole tones (C_1 to D_1, D_1 to E_1, F_1 to G_1, G_1 to A_1, and A_1 to B_1) interrupted by two semitones (E_1 to F_1 and B_1 to C_2) necessitated by the preservation of the fourth, the fifth, and the octave. Pythagoras' diatonic scale seems to be identical to the major scale discussed previously, with five whole steps, or whole tones, and two half steps, or semitones. Use the frequency ratios to figure out the frequencies of the notes in the Pythagorean A-major scale, starting at A_3, which has a frequency of 220 Hz, and compare them to the frequencies of the notes in the even-tempered A-major scale.

Frequencies of Notes in A-Major Scales

	A_3	B_3	$C_4\sharp$	D_4	E_4	$F_4\sharp$	$G_4\sharp$	A_4
Even-tempered	220.0	246.9	277.2	293.7	329.6	370.0	415.3	440.0
Pythagorean	220.0	247.5	278.4	293.3	330.0	371.3	417.7	440.0

Oddly enough, some minor differences emerge between the frequencies of the notes in the two scales. The difference in the frequency ratios is quite obvious when they're given in decimal form:

	Do	*Re*	*Mi*	*Fa*	*Sol*	*La*	*Ti*	*Do*
Even-tempered	f	$1.122f$	$1.26f$	$1.335f$	$1.498f$	$1.682f$	$1.888f$	$2f$
Pythagorean	f	$1.125f$	$1.266f$	$1.333f$	$1.5f$	$1.688f$	$1.898f$	$2f$

A whole tone in the Pythagorean diatonic scale is not quite the same as a whole tone in the major scale. The semitones in the two scales are not the same, either.

	whole tone	semitone
Even-tempered	$2^{\frac{1}{6}} \approx 1.122$	$2^{\frac{1}{12}} \approx 1.0595$
Pythagorean	$\frac{9}{8} = 1.125$	$\frac{256}{243} \approx 1.0535$

In both cases, however, the frequencies (five whole tones and two semitones) "fit" within an octave.

Even-tempered: $\left(2^{\frac{1}{6}}\right)^5 \left(2^{\frac{1}{12}}\right)^2 = 2^{\frac{5}{6}} \cdot 2^{\frac{1}{6}} = 2$

Pythagorean: $\left(\dfrac{9}{8}\right)^5 \left(\dfrac{256}{243}\right)^2 = \dfrac{3{,}869{,}835{,}264}{1{,}934{,}917{,}632} = 2$

But in the Pythagorean diatonic scale, a whole tone is not made up of two semitones, as it is in the even-tempered scale. The result is that the diatonic scale sounds different in different keys— the intervals between notes in the scale are not consistent.

Consider, for example, a D-major scale played on a piano tuned to Pythagorean intervals.

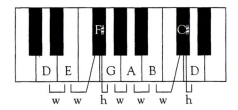

You need to figure out the frequency ratio for G, which was not included in the A-major scale. To get G on the monochord, start with A and go up ten fifths and down five octaves.

$$G = \left(\dfrac{3}{2}\right)^{10} \left(\dfrac{1}{2}\right)^{5} f = \dfrac{3^{10}}{2^{15}} f$$

$$\underset{\substack{\text{up 10}\\\text{fifths}}}{\uparrow} \qquad \underset{\substack{\text{down 5}\\\text{octaves}}}{\downarrow}$$

The frequency ratio between G and F♯ (the fourth and third notes in the D-major scale) should be that of a Pythagorean semitone: 256 : 243 = 1.05. But it's actually slightly larger. It is calculated using a frequency ratio of 27/16 for F♯ (up three fifths and down one octave from A).

$$\frac{G}{F\sharp} = \frac{\dfrac{3^{10}}{2^{15}}}{\dfrac{27}{16}} \approx 1.07$$

And the frequency ratio between A and G (the fifth and fourth notes in the D-major scale) should be that of a Pythagorean whole tone: $9:8 = 1.125$. But it's actually slightly smaller:

$$\frac{A}{G} = \frac{\dfrac{2}{1}}{\dfrac{3^{10}}{2^{15}}} \approx 1.11$$

To summarize, the differences in the frequency ratios for the A- and D-major scales are as follows:

Key of A		. . . compared to . . .		Key of D
		(PYTHAGOREAN FREQ.)		
A				D
	↦ 1.125	=	1.125 ↤	
B				E
	↦ 1.125	=	1.125 ↤	
C♯				F♯
	↦ 1.05	<	1.07 ↤	
D				G
	↦ 1.125	>	1.11 ↤	
E				A
	↦ 1.125	=	1.125 ↤	
F♯				B
	↦ 1.125	=	1.125 ↤	
G♯				C♯
	↦ 1.05	=	1.05 ↤	
A				D

Compare the frequency ratios of the A- and G-major scales. First find the frequency ratio for C (up nine fifths and down four octaves from A).

$$C = \left(\frac{3}{2}\right)^9 \left(\frac{1}{2}\right)^4 f = \frac{3^9}{2^{13}} f$$

up 9   down 4
fifths   octaves

The frequency ratio between C and B (the fourth and third notes in the G-major scale), using a frequency ratio of 9/8 for B (up two fifths and down one octave from A), should be $256:243 = 1.05$—a Pythagorean semitone. But it's actually slightly larger.

$$\frac{C}{B} = \frac{\frac{3^9}{2^{13}}}{\frac{9}{8}} \approx 1.07$$

And the frequency ratio between D and C (the fifth and fourth notes in the G-major scale), using a frequency ratio of 4/3 for D (up one fourth from A), should be $9:8 = 1.125$—a Pythagorean whole tone. But it's actually slightly smaller.

$$\frac{D}{C} = \frac{\frac{4}{3}}{\frac{3^9}{2^{13}}} \approx 1.11$$

This time, the summary shows that four of the frequency ratios are different—the two semitones are smaller, and two of the whole tones are larger, as shown on the following page.

Key of A		...compared to...		Key of G
		(PYTHAGOREAN FREQ.)		
A				G
	↦ 1.125	>	1.11 ↤	
B				A
	↦ 1.125	=	1.125 ↤	
C♯				B
	↦ 1.05	<	1.07 ↤	
D				C
	↦ 1.125	>	1.11 ↤	
E				D
	↦ 1.125	=	1.125 ↤	
F♯				E
	↦ 1.125	=	1.125 ↤	
G♯				F♯
	↦ 1.05	<	1.07 ↤	
A				G

The differences between frequency ratios in the A-major and C-major scales are as follows:

Key of A		...compared to...		Key of C
		(PYTHAGOREAN FREQ.)		
A				C
	↦ 1.125	>	1.11 ↤	
B				D
	↦ 1.125	=	1.125 ↤	
C♯				E
	↦ 1.05	<	1.07 ↤	
D				F
	↦ 1.125	=	1.125 ↤	
E				G
	↦ 1.125	>	1.1 ↤	
F♯				A
	↦ 1.125	=	1.125 ↤	
G♯				B
	↦ 1.05	<	1.07 ↤	
A				C

Each major scale has its own set of intervals. Therefore, you cannot readily switch between keys, or transpose, on an instrument tuned with Pythagorean tuning, for some intervals will inevitably sound out of tune. For playing chords and modulating from key to key, it is a completely unsatisfactory tuning, since the ratios between two notes of a scale will be different in different keys.

Why, then, was this method of tuning the preferred method for so many years? First of all, much of the music composed and played during the time Pythagorean tuning was employed was simpler and had fewer transpositions and modulations than the music of today. Remember, also, that integer ratios were thought to be inherently the most perfect. In addition to being pure and neat, these intervals are extremely convenient in the geometric sense. Since the ratios can be expressed using integers, they can be represented by measurable line segments. Therefore, a geometrically accurate monochord can easily be constructed as a reference for the Pythagorean tuning.

A primitive instrument, with a string to represent each note in the Pythagorean diatonic scale, would look like this:

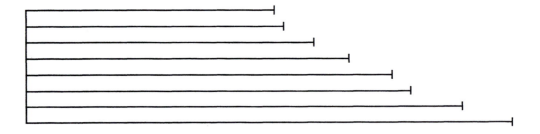

This simple instrument would be very easy to tune. The only requirement is that the string lengths (and, therefore, the frequencies) are in the correct ratios.

What if the intervals could be expressed only by using irrational numbers like $\sqrt{2}$ or $\sqrt{3}$? An irrational number cannot be expressed as a fraction—its decimal portion neither repeats not terminates. Therefore, a line segment that is $\sqrt{2}$ centimeters long, for example, could never be measured completely accurately. One would always have to approximate the decimal and, therefore, the length. A monochord constructed using string lengths involving irrational numbers would produce only approximate pitches. Granted, the error would be indistinguishable to the ear, but it would exist nonetheless.

There is an interesting difficulty inherent in Pythagorean tuning. Note that on the piano there are 12 fifths in the same space as 7 octaves.

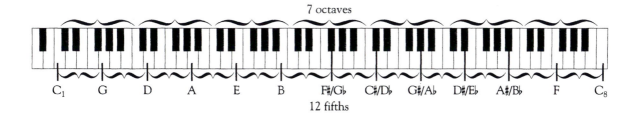

After moving up 12 fifths, we arrive back at the same note on which we started, 7 octaves higher, with each note of the chromatic scale represented once. This cycle technically continues forever in both directions, and is often referred to as the **circle of fifths**, shown below. C and G are in the interval of a fifth, as are F and C, B♭ and F, and so on.

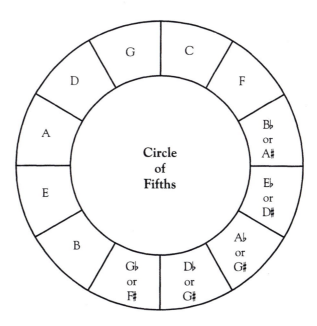

Therefore, we should be able to obtain the frequency ratio between C_8 and C_1 in one of two ways, either by adding 12 fifths, or by adding 7 octaves. Using the even-tempered ratios, there's no problem.

$$7 \text{ Octaves} = 2^7 = 128 \left.\phantom{\begin{matrix}a\\b\end{matrix}}\right\} \text{SAME}$$
$$12 \text{ Fifths} = \left(2^{\frac{7}{12}}\right)^{12} = 2^7 = 128$$

But try the same thing using the Pythagorean ratios:

$$7 \text{ Octaves} = 2^7 = 128 \left.\phantom{\begin{matrix}a\\b\end{matrix}}\right\} \text{DIFFERENT!}$$
$$12 \text{ Fifths} = \left(\frac{3}{2}\right)^{12} = 129.7463379...$$

The frequency ratios in this case are different! It seems as though 12 fifths reach farther than 7 octaves. If you were using a monochord and Pythagorean ratios to find C_8, you'd get a slightly higher note if you successively cut the string length by two thirds 12 times than you would if you cut it in half 7 times.

The amount by which 12 fifths overshoot 7 octaves is called the **Pythagorean comma.**

$$\frac{\left(\frac{3}{2}\right)^{12}}{2^7} = 1.013643265...$$

Pythagorean Comma

The instruments of ancient Greece usually had little more than one octave, but this mathematical inconsistency still existed. There are six whole tones within the space of one octave. Therefore, one should be able to obtain C* from C (move up an octave) on a monochord either by shortening the string to half its length to double the frequency, or by successively shortening the string to eight ninths of its length six times to move up six whole tones.

$$1 \text{ Octave} = 2 \left.\phantom{\begin{matrix}a\\b\end{matrix}}\right\} \quad \frac{\left(\frac{9}{8}\right)^6}{2} = 1.013643265...$$
$$6 \text{ Whole Tones} = \left(\frac{9}{8}\right)^6 = 2.02728653...$$

Once again, the Pythagorean comma appears! It turns out that any tuning method using ratios of integers produces tone spirals, not tone cycles. How can this be? And which C* is correct?

The explanation for the confusing Pythagorean comma is that the Pythagorean fifth takes up a little bit more of the octave than the fifth obtained by dividing the octave evenly into 12 parts.

$$\text{Pythagorean Fifth} \quad = \frac{3}{2} \quad = 1.5$$

$$\text{Even-Tempered Fifth} \quad = 2^{\frac{7}{12}} = 1.4983...$$

Equal temperament does away with the Pythagorean comma, and can be explained as follows:

> Temperament is an attempt to reconcile two conflicting musical norms. One is the octave, which sets a definite, frame-like limit. The other is the bypassing of the octave by the accumulation of any other primary, scale-building interval. Temperament is the musical way of fitting an otherwise endless series into a definite space.[11]

The transition from Pythagorean tuning to equal temperament took centuries, and paralleled the changing relationship between mathematics and music. In the time of the ancient Greeks, the Pythagoreans developed a division of the curriculum, later dubbed the *quadrivium*. Within the quadrivium, shown on the following page, music was a strictly mathematical discipline, dealing with number relationships, ratios, and proportions.

The quadrivium eventually evolved into the seven *artes liberales* with the addition of the *trivium* (grammar, rhetoric, and logic), but music's position as a subset of mathematics remained constant throughout the Middle Ages. Young people spent nine or ten years studying the often tedious mathematics of the Pythagorean musical tradition, without ever focusing on musical creation or performance! There is little known about the folk music of this time period.

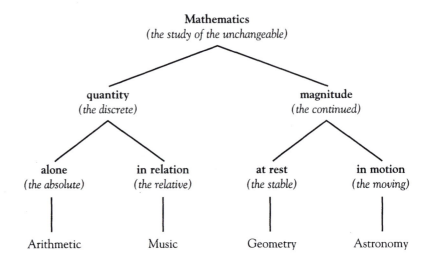

Quadrivium

Mathematics
(the study of the unchangeable)

quantity
(the discrete)

magnitude
(the continued)

alone
(the absolute)

in relation
(the relative)

at rest
(the stable)

in motion
(the moving)

Arithmetic

Music

Geometry

Astronomy

The longevity of the Pythagorean musical tradition was aided by Boethius, a philosopher born in Rome in about A.D. 480, who was the main translator of classical music theory in the Middle Ages. He believed that music and the proportions that represented musical intervals were inextricably entwined with morality and human nature, and preferred Pythagorean ratios. Boethius wrote a rather unusual definition of a *musician*:

> That person is a musician, who, through careful rational contemplation, has gained the knowledge of making music, not through the slavery of labor, but through the sovereignty of reason.[12]

By today's standards, this is a completely preposterous definition of a musician, since performers and composers aren't even included.

The narrow medieval conceptions of music and musicians, along with the strict doctrines of the Church, the prevailing educational system, and the general lack of acceptance of irrational numbers, created an atmosphere in which musical development was hampered and only Pythagorean tuning was used for 15 centuries. How could music evolve if the only goal was to understand the mathematical relationships between tones?

During the twelfth century, the composers and players of music (who were not musicians, according to Boethius) began to break away from the Pythagorean tradition and the stodgy mathematics it represented, creating new styles and types of music. A new division of the sciences was created, called scholastic divinity, that did not specifically include music. The monophonic Gregorian chant slowly evolved into polyphonic music with several instruments and voices. The performance of more complex compositions necessitated experimentation with alternate tunings and temperaments.

The tuning experiments resulted in variations on Pythagorean tuning, such as equal temperament and something called **Just tuning,** which is based on the octave $(2:1)$, the pure fifth $(3:2)$, and the pure major third $(5:4)$, resulting in eight pure thirds. The chart on the following page shows how Just tuning compares to Pythagorean tuning and even-tempered tuning.

The new tunings still used mathematics in the calculation of the interval ratios, but the mathematics was no longer dictated solely by Pythagorean principles. And mathematics was now used in a practical way to get the desired tuning results—it was a means to an end, not an end to be mastered above all other ends.

This change in attitude about the relationship between mathematics and music caused an ongoing disagreement between the mathematicians, who wanted strict adherence to their complicated formulas (which were first applied to the monochord, and then to the instrument), and the musicians, who wanted tuning rules that were easy to apply.[13] In fact, many musicians began to rely more on their ears and less on the cumbersome monochord. Equal temperament didn't become truly popular until the 1630s, when Father Mersenne formulated invaluable rules for tuning by beats that are still used today.[14]

By the eighteenth century, musicians such as Johann Sebastian Bach were tuning their instruments using equal temperament. The complexity of range and modulation in Bach's music necessitated it. He wrote *The Well-Tempered Clavichord*, consisting of major and minor pieces in each key, to demonstrate the possibilities for modulation created by an equal tuning.[15]

	Pythagorean		Just		Even-Tempered	
Frequency Ratios	f	(f)	f	(f)	f	(f)
	$\frac{9}{8}f$	$(1.125f)$	$\frac{9}{8}f$	$(1.125f)$	$2^{\frac{1}{6}}f$	$(1.122f)$
	$\frac{81}{64}f$	$(1.266f)$	$\frac{5}{4}f$	$(1.25f)$	$2^{\frac{1}{3}}f$	$(1.260f)$
	$\frac{4}{3}f$	$(1.333f)$	$\frac{4}{3}f$	$(1.333f)$	$2^{\frac{5}{12}}f$	$(1.335f)$
	$\frac{3}{2}f$	$(1.5f)$	$\frac{3}{2}f$	$(1.5f)$	$2^{\frac{7}{12}}f$	$(1.498f)$
	$\frac{27}{16}f$	$(1.688f)$	$\frac{5}{3}f$	$(1.67f)$	$2^{\frac{3}{4}}f$	$(1.682f)$
	$\frac{243}{128}f$	$(1.898f)$	$\frac{15}{8}f$	$(1.875f)$	$2^{\frac{11}{12}}f$	$(1.888f)$
	$2f$	$(2f)$	$2f$	$(2f)$	$2f$	$(2f)$
(A-major scale) Frequencies (in Hz)	220.0		220.0		220.0	
	247.5		247.5		246.9	
	278.4		275.0		277.2	
	293.3		293.3		293.7	
	330.0		330.3		329.6	
	371.3		366.7		370.0	
	417.7		412.5		415.3	
	440.0		440.0		440.0	

Throughout history, mathematics has both thwarted and aided musical progress. The changing conception of what a musician is reflects the changing relationship between mathematics and music. Centuries ago, a musician was one who studied the mathematical relationships underlying the tonal relationships and judged music using reason rather than the ear. Today, a musician is anyone who writes or makes music, whether or not they have a theoretical understanding of the mathematics behind it. Yet even though music is no longer a strictly mathematical discipline, mathematics will forever be inherent in music, and will continue to influence the evolution of music theory.

CHAPTER 5

THE SONG

THE COMPOSITION OF an enduring piece of music can be likened to the design of a classic painting or of a well-coordinated garden. It is not unlike the engineering of a sturdy bridge or of a functional, well-proportioned building. There is an underlying structure in all these cases that is influenced by mathematics, sometimes more obviously than others, and sometimes more deliberately than others on the part of the artist, designer, engineer, or composer.

A basic procedure for achieving cohesion in a piece of music is the restating of a sequence of tones again and again—in variations, of course, to avoid monotony and to give the composition character. Care must be taken to assure that the transformed restatements are pleasing to the ear and interesting to the mind. If done well, these variations will help to make the musical piece more easily remembered. This will give it broader, more lasting appeal, since the recognition of repetitive phrases is important to musical pleasure. Some of the techniques used to give a composition unity without making it boring are grounded in plane geometry.

Musical transformations are closely related to the four basic geometric transformations. A **geometric transformation** relocates a rigid geometric figure in the plane while carefully preserving its size and shape. The original configuration is not distorted by the manipulation.

The first and most simple of these geometric transformations is **translation.** The following diagram gives an example of a geometric translation. Each point on the triangle is moved a defined distance along a course parallel to the path of every other point . The result is a relocation of the triangle with exactly the same size, shape, and orientation as the original triangle.

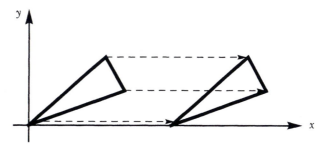

If musical notes are placed at the vertices of the triangle,

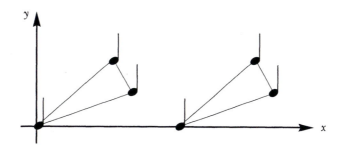

and then these notes are transferred to a musical staff,

the musical counterpart of the geometric translation emerges.

The most simple musical application of the translation is a **repeat,** such as the one that occurs in the spiritual *When the Saints Go Marching In.* (This repeated sequence of notes is the **theme** of this song.) The sequence of notes simply appears intact at another location in time. This can be shown in formal musical notation:

The repetition of the sequence can also be informally sketched. The sketches can be represented by equations $y = f(x)$, $y = f(x-1)$, $y = f(x-2)$.

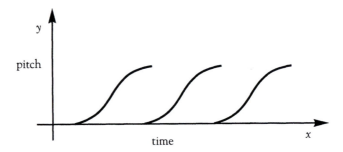

Sketch of the translation that occurs in *When the Saints Go Marching In.*

The popular round *Row, Row, Row Your Boat* sung in harmony provides another example of a translation that is nothing more than a repeat, though an overlapping one with respect to time:

Row Row Row Your Boat

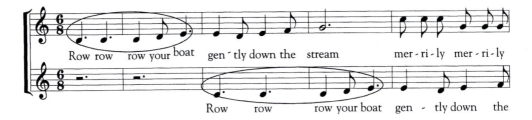

The overlapping repeat in *Row, Row, Row Your Boat* is sketched geometrically as follows:

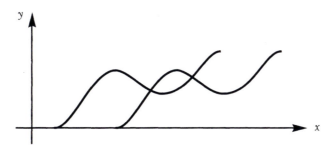

Geometric translations are not necessarily strictly horizontal; a geometric figure could also be raised or lowered, and would still have a musical counterpart:

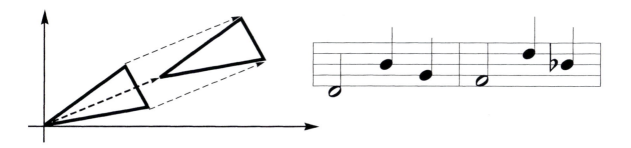

Transposition, a more sophisticated application of translation to music, involves the movement of an exact sequence of notes to another location on the scale (and, typically, another location in time, also). An example of this is the theme from *Yankee Doodle:*

Yan - kee Doo - dle   keep it up   Yan - kee Doo - dle   dan - dy.

Notice that the imitated sequence is transposed downward. The equations of these sketches could be $y = f(x)$ and $y = f(x - 1) - 1$.

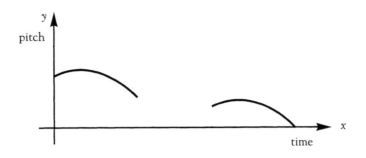

Sketch of the translation that occurs in *Yankee Doodle*.

Another example of downward transposition can be found in the famous German carol *O Christmas Tree*.

O Christ-mas tree, O Christ-mas tree! Your col-or is un - chang - ing.

When from all trees the col-ors go, You still are green a - midst the snow.

The second geometric transformation is **reflection.** When a geometric figure is reflected across a line, its mirror image appears on the other side. Each point on the reflected figure is the same distance from the line of reflection as its mirrored point in the original figure. And the paths of reflection of all points are parallel.

Geometric reflection

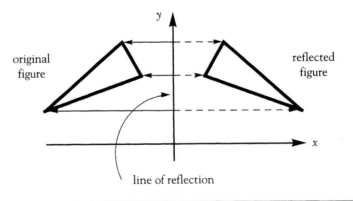

The musical counterpart of a horizontal reflection (across the *y*-axis) is called **retrogression,** notated below:

Exact reflections occur frequently in music, though they are not as easily discernible to the ear as translations. A clear simple reflection can be found in the song *Raindrops Keep Falling on My Head.* The equations of the corresponding sketches could be $y = f(x)$ and $y = f(-x)$.

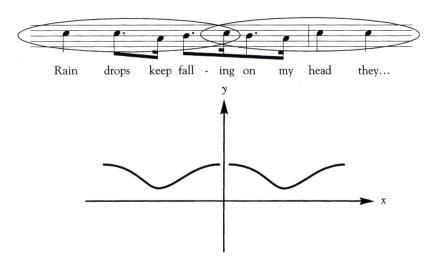

Another example can be found in the Shaker tune *Simple Gifts*.

A geometric reflection across the *x*-axis is much the same except that the line of reflection is horizontal rather than vertical.

Its musical counterpart is called **inversion** and can take several forms. One occurs in harmony:

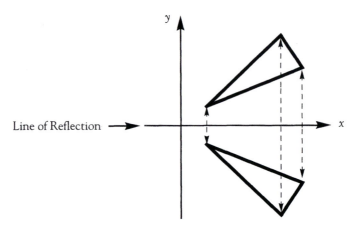

The equations for these sketches might be $y = f(x)$ and $y = -f(x)$.

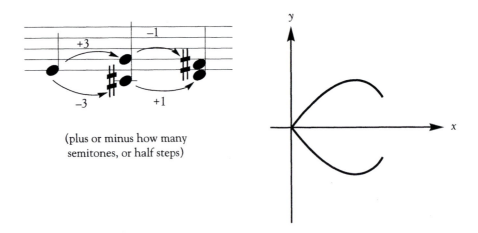

(plus or minus how many semitones, or half steps)

The other form of inversion occurs in melody and can be found in the beloved Old English tune *Greensleeves:*

A - las my Love you do me wrong To cast me off dis - court - eous - ly

This is actually an example of the third geometric transformation, called **glide reflection,** which is a combination of two transformations—a translation followed by a reflection.

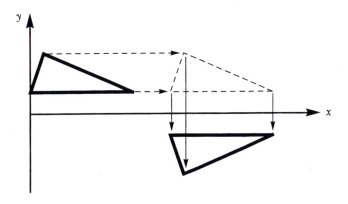

The musical counterpart and sketches might be represented by equations in the form $y = f(x)$ and $y = -f(x-1)$.

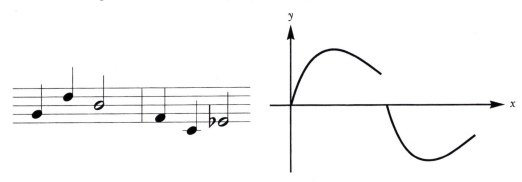

An approximation of this kind of inversion can be found in the popular Spanish song *Guantanamera:*

Guan - ta - na - mer - a,   gua - ji - ra   Guan - ta - na - mer - a
My   in - spi - ra - tion,   Guan - ta - na - mo's fair - est la - dy.

Close examination reveals that this inversion is not exact. Imitation in musical composition may be strict (the duplication of a sequence, following note for note the course laid out by the leading sequence), but an absolute adherence to this is not as necessary as it may seem. Approximate or free imitation, in which the composer takes some liberties with the original sequence, can still convey an unmistakable sense of unity and cohesion. The inversion in *Guantanamera* is an excellent example of free imitation that works beautifully. Approximations are also often necessitated by the lyrics, or by the need for emphasis or minor alterations of rhythm.

The fourth geometric transformation, **rotation,** occurs when a geometric figure is rotated 180 degrees about a point and repositioned.

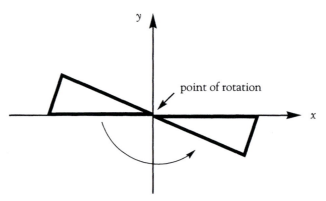

This can also be achieved by reflecting the figure across both axes in turn, in any order.

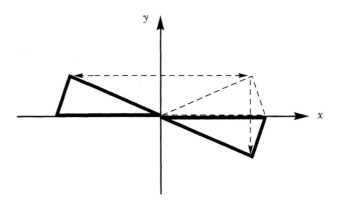

Inasmuch as horizontal musical reflection (across the y-axis) is retrogression, and vertical reflection (across the x-axis) is inversion, the musical counterpart of rotation is appropriately called **retrograde inversion.** The equations of corresponding sketches might be $y = f(x)$ and $y = -f(-x)$.

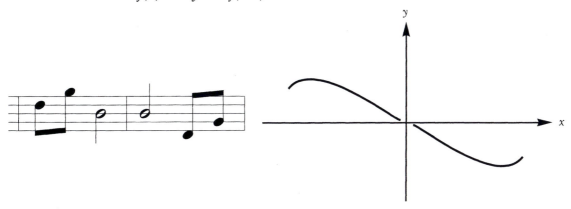

An example of retrograde inversion is clearly evident in a type of music called **serial music.** In the early twentieth century, Arnold Schoenberg introduced a new type of music based on a series of 12 notes (hence the name *serial music*). The 12 notes are the 12 semitones of the chromatic scale. They can appear in any order; however, it is critical that no note in the basic series is repeated until all the other 11 notes of that series have been played. To avoid unmerciful monotony, the basic configuration of the series is established and then transformed using retrogression (geometric reflection), inversion (geometric glide reflection) and retrograde inversion (geometric rotation).

Consider, for example, this basic 12-note tone row:

This is the same basic tone row **inverted** (upside-down, or reflected across the *x*-axis):

Let's go back again to the original basic 12-note tone row:

This is the same basic tone row in **retrogression** (reflected horizontally across the y-axis).

If the same basic 12-note tone row is reflected first across one axis and then across the other, it is called **retrograde inversion** and is like a **rotation.**

Basic Tone Row

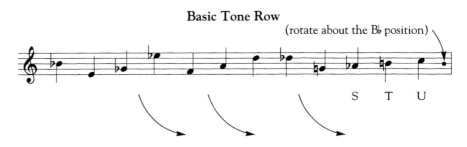

Basic Tone Row in Retrograde - Inversion

The basic geometry involved here isn't the only interesting mathematics that emerges in a study of serial music. For any established sequence, a tone row can begin on any one of those 12 notes. Since there are four transformations (original, retrograde, inversion, and retrograde inversion), there are 48 (12×4) variations on any one sequence of twelve notes. An entire three-hour opera has been written using the same sequence of 12 notes in a tone row!

The establishing of a basic sequence, however, can be done in 12! ways (that is, $12 \times 11 \times 10 \times \ldots \times 3 \times 2 \times 1$ ways, or a total of 479,001,600 ways). This is because there are 12 different tones in the chromatic scale from which notes can be sequentially selected. In spite of all this apparent potential variety, serial music has never really become popular because of its fundamentally atonal quality.

But the classical, enduring music of the Renaissance (c. 1300–1600) is replete with musical transformations. Nowhere are they more plentiful or pleasingly obvious than in the fugues written by Johann Sebastian Bach. A **fugue** is defined for children as a "musical piece based on a short tune or theme which appears constantly throughout, though sometimes upside down, right side up, slowed down, speeded up or backwards," simple words for musical transformations.[16] Bach's *The Well-Tempered Clavichord*, consisting of 48 preludes and fugues, includes many musical transformations.

FUGUE II

Combinations of musical transformations characterize some well-known tunes, including *Londonderry Air, My Country Tis of Thee,* and *Joy to the World,* the latter starting out with something of an eight-note tone row.

A dazzling array of transposition, retrogression, inversion and retrograde inversion occurs in this incredible piece of music attributed to Wolfgang Amadeus Mozart.

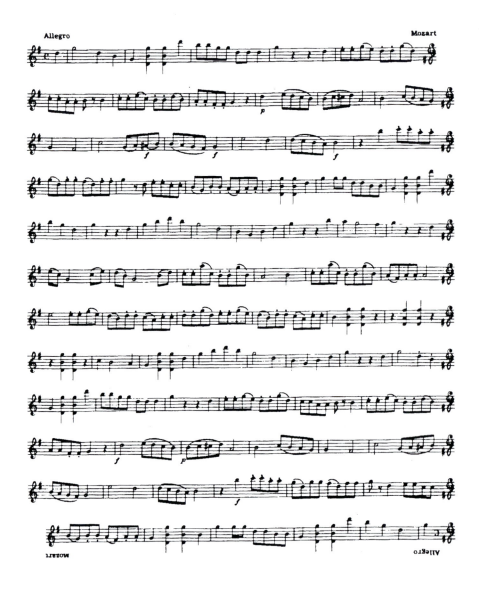

It is intended to be placed flat on a table with two musicians sitting directly opposite each other, positioned on the two ends of the composition. Each musician begins at the top of the sheet as he or she views it and works down to the bottom. Each is reading the other's line upside down, but at all times the music fits together as a duet. Since there are an even number of rows, they are never playing the same row at the same time.

More of the same can be found in Mozart's *Melody Dicer*, written as a dice game. The player has the opportunity to compose a waltz consisting of 16 bars, but the exact composition of each bar is determined by the roll of the dice. Mozart composed 11 different options (corresponding to the numbers 2 to 12 that could turn up on a pair of dice) for each of 14 of the bars, 2 options for one of bars, and the final bar was fixed. There are, therefore, 2×11^{14} (over 750 trillion) variations on this waltz, only a tiny fraction of which have ever been heard! Here is the blank sheet on which the composition is to be written, along with Mozart's options for 2 of the bars:

Blank on which to compose

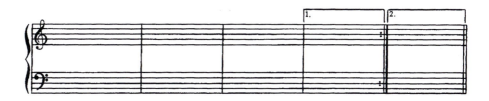

The geometry of some musical compositions bears a close relationship to the architecture of the buildings in which they were to be heard. One notable example is a motet (a type of choral composition) entitled *Nuper Rosarum Flores* composed for the dedication of the Santa Maria del Fiore cathedral in Florence, Italy, on March 25, 1436. The architect of the cathedral was Filippo Brunelleschi, and the composer of the music was Guillarume Dufay.

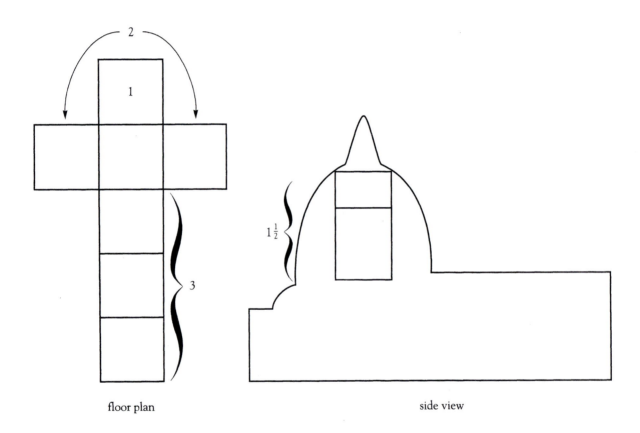

floor plan

side view

The critical proportions of the interior of the cathedral are based on whole number ratios, in keeping with Brunelleschi's plan for the harmonic organization of space. A square is the basic unit of the cathedral, whose floor plan is a cross. The extremities of the cross are the altar area (one square), the transepts (two squares) and the main corridor (three squares). One and a half times the area of that same square defines the interior of the dome of the cathedral. These ratios, $3:2:1:1\frac{1}{2}$, are the equivalent of the whole number ratios $6:4:2:3$.

These same proportions $(6:4:2:3)$ were used in the composition of the motet such that specific sections of the music correspond to specific parts of the interior of the cathedral, as seen in the preceding illustration. Furthermore, both the architecture of the building and the structure of the motet rely heavily on the number 7, considered the "holy number" in ancient number symbolism.

Number symbolism (called *gematria*) has been identified in other musical compositions, especially those of Johann Sebastian Bach. Certain mystical attributes are assigned to certain numbers, and when those numbers undergird a composition, they provide a link between music and meaning. Following is a sampling of such numbers and some of their associated meanings in sacred music of the early 1700s:

3 - Members of the Trinity
4 - Gospels
6 - Days of Creation
7 - Sacraments, Holy Spirit
10 - Commandments
12 - Apostles, tribes of Israel

The number of bars in some of Bach's compositions was directly connected to these meanings. Whenever he put six pieces together under one title (*Six English Pieces, Six French Suites*, the *Six Brandenburg Concertos*) he was paying homage to the six days in which, according to Judeo-Christian belief, the Lord created the universe. His *B Minor Mass* is 49 bars in length (7×7 = Holy, Holy) and *Patrem Omnipotentem* is 84 (7×12 = Holy Apostles) bars long.

The numbers 84 and 14 are especially important in Bach's compositions for several reasons. If the alphabet is aligned with the natural numbers so that $A = 1$, $B = 2$, $C = 3$, and so on, then the name *Bach* is represented by the number 14 ($\mathbf{B}(2) + \mathbf{A}(1) + \mathbf{C}(3) + \mathbf{H}(8) = 14$). Furthermore, 14×6 (for the 6 days of Creation) $= 84$.

In addition to having 84 bars in many of his compositions, Bach sometimes wrote the number 84 at the end of his pieces, which confirmed the significance he attached to the number.

An examination of the mathematics of musical composition should include certain unique selections. An example is the composition by Brazilian composer Villa-Lobos for three **metronomes** (a device for fixing the speed at which a piece of music is to be played) ticking at different speeds. This would provide a magnificent study in least common multiples! Gyorgy Ligeti composed a piece for 100 metronomes ticking just out of time with one another that provides an excellent opportunity to study probability (the probability that any two metronomes would ever tick together!)

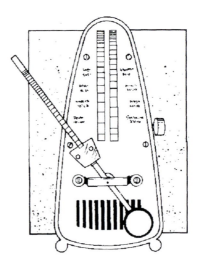

Then there is American composer John Cage's famous and provocative 4'33". It consists of exactly 4 minutes and 33 seconds of silence, divided into three movements titled Part I, Part II, and Part III. It has been suggested that this piece reflects the composer's creative philosophy that virtually every kind of sound is potentially musical. On the other hand, perhaps it simply reflects the composer's sense of humor!

In England there is a long-established art and cherished tradition called Change-Ringing that has interesting mathematical implications. In small towns, occasions of joy or sadness were marked by the ringing of descending scales over and over on church bells. Some ringers, in the interest of alleviating boredom, would change the sequence in which bells were rung, giving the practice its name, **Change-Ringing.**

The number of bells varies from about 5 to 12. If a church has 5 bells, there are 5! (or 120) different arrangements in which they could be rung. Ringing at a rate of about 144 notes per minute, a **full peal** (in this case, 120 arrangements times 5 notes in each arrangement, totaling 600 notes) could be rung in a little over 4 minutes. With 6 bells, the 720 different arrangements would take about 30 minutes to ring. With 8 bells, a full peal would take about a day and a half, ringing around the clock. With 10 bells, it would take about half a year. With 12 bells, it would take about 76 years, working day and night, to ring a full peal of all the arrangements of the bell tones.

The mathematics of Change-Ringing is actually much more complex than this. Because of the gymnastics required to play the heavy church bells, there are rules governing the sequential ringing of certain pairs of bells; some pairs aren't allowed because it would be too difficult to accomplish. The numbers change considerably when this consideration is factored in.

As can be clearly seen, musical composition—whether traditional or avant garde, deliberate or casual—is closely related to and undergirded by numbers and geometry.

CHAPTER 6

THE SOURCE

MUSICAL INSTRUMENTS ARE mechanical devices that create specific vibrations that are interpreted by our ears as differing musical sounds. In most cases, something quite simple sets up the initial vibrations. These vibrations are then transmitted to something more substantial that acts as a resonator to amplify the vibrations and transmit them through the air to our ears.

With most musical instruments, the initial vibrations originate in one of three ways. The first is the vibration of a string caused by the bowing, plucking, or striking of it. The second is the vibration of a column of air in a tube of metal or wood. The third is the vibration of some unit of membrane, parchment, wood, metal, or other substance by striking or pounding. Musical instruments are generally divided into three categories based on the way sound is produced on them. The three categories are stringed instruments, wind instruments, and percussion instruments.

In the case of stringed instruments, consider the violin. The initial vibrations are generated by a string set in motion by the player's finger or bow. On its own, a string would make very little audible sound because it is too thin to move enough air around to create vibrations strong enough to be heard. But the vibrations of the string are transmitted to the wooden body of the instrument through a small structure called a **bridge.** The body of a violin is just light enough to be set in motion by the string, but stiff enough to push on the surrounding air sufficiently to set strong sound waves going. It is the wooden body of the violin that generates the vibrations of air that are heard, but the strings get the body of the violin moving—with the help of the bridge.

Bridge

Although their designs differ, as does the manner in which they are played, all **stringed instruments** work basically the same way. Strings produce different sounds depending on thickness (the thinner the string, the higher the note), tension (the tighter the string, the higher the note) and length (the shorter the length, the higher the note).

The structure that functions like the bridge differs, and numbers of strings differ; the trumpet marine has only one string while the classical harp has 47 strings. Stringed instruments of one kind or other can be found in virtually every culture.

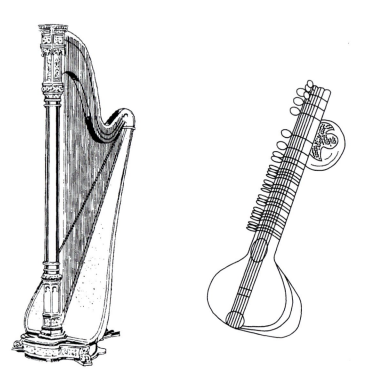

Wind instruments fall into two main categories: woodwinds and brass, so named after the traditional materials of their construction. The materials are no longer an absolute distinction between the two, but the method of changing the size of the vibrating column of air certainly is.

In **woodwinds,** holes are bored into the tube in which a column of air vibrates. Only the air between the mouthpiece and the first open hole vibrates, so that distance determines the length of the column. The shorter the distance (all the holes open), the shorter the column and the higher the note. When all the holes are closed and the vibrating air comes out the bell at the end of the instrument, the lowest possible note is produced. In some woodwinds, such as the flute and piccolo, the breath alone activates the column of air. In others, such as the clarinet and saxophone, the breath activates one or two reeds that activate the column of air.

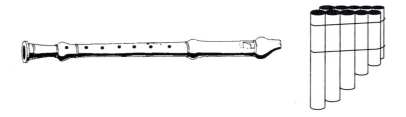

In the case of **brass instruments,** the length of the air column is determined by the length of the tube, which can be changed. There are no holes in the tube of a brass instrument. On a trombone, the length of the tube is changed quite visibly by moving the slide. The vibration of the lips activates the column of air, and blowing harder or softer can further change the pitch of the notes.

On a French horn, the same thing is accomplished by using valves.

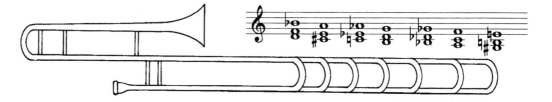

The different settings of a trombone slide coordinate with different chords.

Air always goes in the mouthpiece and out the horn at the end, but it may travel a short (high note) or long (low note) distance before emerging. On brass instruments, the player can produce the harmonics of the lowest tone produced with a given valve fingering or slide position by changing the tension of his or her lips.

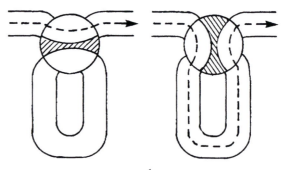

rotary valves

The sound produced by the human voice, the oldest and most basic musical instrument, is created by a vibrating column of air originating in the lungs, passing through the voice box (larynx) and out through the mouth. On each side of the larynx are two vocal cords through which the air column must pass. We can control the degree to which these cords are opened or closed, which will determine the tone made by the column of air passing through them. A wide opening allows a wide column of air to pass through, making a low note; a narrow opening makes a higher note.

The size of the vocal cords also affects the sound because longer cords allow a larger air column through and produce a lower note. The average size of women's vocal cords is a little over 1 centimeter (11 millimeters); children's, less than 1 centimeter (8 millimeters); and men's, about 1.5 centimeters (15 millimeters). The difference in these dimensions explains why men usually have lower voices than women (longer cords), and children have higher voices than women (shorter cords).

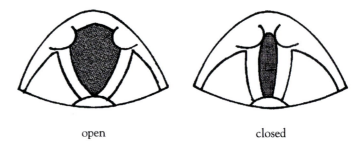

open   closed

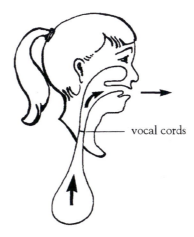

Vocal Cords:

Longer = larger column of air
(lower sound—men)

Shorter = smaller column of air
(higher sound—children)

The vocal cords themselves act something like reeds in reed instruments; the structures and cavities in the head (skull, sinuses, nose, and so on) act as amplifiers or resonators. Different usage of these spaces creates different styles of singing. An opera singer may talk about using his or her "chest voice," or feeling the sound resonate in the forehead. In much traditional Native American singing, the vibration is felt only in the throat, never in the roof of the mouth.

Percussion instruments are perhaps the easiest to understand because they produce sound simply by being struck. There are many different kinds of percussion instruments, including a vast array of gadgets that produce special effects.

Some drums can be tuned to different pitches by changing the tension of the skins covering them. Africans have a special drum called the *dundun*, or "variable-pitch talking drum." It's shaped like an hourglass and has two heads laced together. When these strings are squeezed under the arm, the tension of the head changes and the pitch of the tone created when it is hit gets higher or lower. A talented drummer can truly make the drum talk!

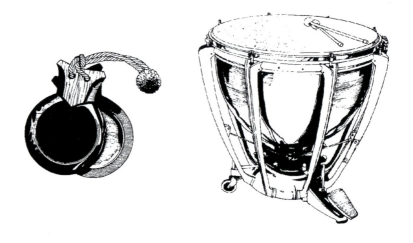

Castanets   Kettledrum

In the case of most percussion instruments, however, different pitches are simply a function of different sizes. All other things being equal, striking a small instrument will produce a higher sound than striking a large one.

Some instruments are not so easy to categorize. Musical saws, jew's-harps, and musical glasses are examples, as are certain keyboard instruments. The keys on the keyboard of an accordion or pipe organ open valves that allow columns of air to flow through pipes of different lengths and widths. These are really wind instruments.

Each key on an electric organ or portable synthesizer completes a different electrical circuit, creating a different sound. In addition, synthesizers have built-in computers so that, by using various knobs and switches, the shape of the basic sound can be changed, creating new sounds. The number of different sounds that can be generated by a synthesizer is virtually limitless.

Pianos have characteristics of both percussion and string instruments; striking a key causes a hammer to hit strings of varying length, width, and tension, thus producing a tone. So, even though they are usually found in the percussion section of an orchestra, pianos are actually stringed instruments, as are harpsichords and clavichords.

You already know that the tone produced by a vibrating string depends on its length. If this were the only thing affecting tone, a piano whose shortest string was 20 centimeters long would have to be over 30 meters long to house the longest string! But the tone produced also depends on the thickness (the thinner the string, the higher the note) and the tension (the tighter the string, the higher the note) of the string.[9] Therefore, even in a concert grand piano the longest string is only just over 2.5 meters long. It is doubly wrapped in wire to make it extra thick, and is positioned along with other base strings over the shorter strings to conserve space (see illustration at the beginning of Chapter 4).

Mickey Hart, one of the drummers for the Grateful Dead, has created an instrument called "the Beam." It is a ten-foot aluminum girder stretched with twelve piano strings tuned in unisons, fifths, and octaves with very low frequencies (around 30 Hz—almost as low as the lowest note on the piano). A magnetic pickup amplifies the vibrations created by plucking, hitting, even kicking the strings. Hart says of his instrument, "You can go lower and deeper with the Beam than with anything else I know, descending into vibrations that are perceived less by the ear than felt as shockwaves throughout the body. There is nothing like a long vibrating string."[17]

THE PEOPLE

WHEN THE HISTORY of mathematics in Western civilization is traced back to its earliest years, the most prominent identifiable individual found is Pythagoras, the Greek philosopher and mathematician. Pythagoras is also uniquely prominent when the history of Western music is traced back to its recorded origins. Indeed, in both cases there is not another individual of comparable distinction or stature. Pythagoras is linked historically to some of the earliest known investigations connecting numbers and musical sounds, which profoundly influenced the development of Western music theory as we know it today. He clearly embodied the earliest recorded human connection between mathematics and music.

As important as his role was believed to be, little accurate information is known about Pythagoras. This is due to several factors, the most significant being that relevant documentation from 500 B.C. is nonexistent now, and may never have been very accurate. Several biographies were written about him in antiquity, including one by Aristotle, but none have survived. The problem is aggravated by the fact that Pythagoras' life and work were shrouded in secrecy—even during his lifetime. Finally, whatever may have been known about him has by now taken on legendary proportions, making it difficult to distinguish history from fantasy.

It is believed that Pythagoras was born on the Greek island of Samos, off the coast of what is now Turkey around the year 580 B.C. A contemporary of both Buddha and Confucius, Pythagoras lived at a critical time in the development of both mathematics and religion and was deeply involved in both. He is believed to have coined the word *mathematics*, which means "that which is learned."

By most accounts, Pythagoras was a student of Thales of Miletus. Thales is frequently referred to as the first true mathematician, and he is definitely the first person in history to whom specific mathematical discoveries were attributed. One of those discoveries is the Theorem of Thales:

Theorem of Thales

An angle inscribed in a semicircle is a right angle.

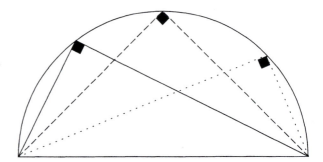

With Thales' encouragement to broaden his horizons, Pythagoras is said to have traveled to Egypt and Mesopotamia, perhaps going as far as India. Then, because of political unrest, he was unable to return to his birthplace. He settled instead at Crotona, on the southeast coast of Italy, where he established an academy devoted to the study of philosophy, mathematics, and natural science. Pythagoras' academy became a closely knit order—something of a semireligious, semimathematical cult with secret rites, mystics, and observances, whose members remained united for life. They were known as the Pythagoreans, and their motto was "All is Number." Though they are sometimes inaccurately referred to as a "brotherhood," it is understood that women were also active participants—most especially Theano, Pythagoras' wife, and two of their daughters.

The Pythagoreans believed that music and math provided keys to the secrets of the world. Their doctrine of the "music of the spheres" held that human souls must be attuned to the laws of the universe; it also suggested that planets and other bodies moving in space produce sounds, that the universe itself virtually sings! Later, Plato (c. 427–347 B.C.) clarified this concept more fully in his profoundly influential writings, *The Republic* and *Timaeus*. The Pythagoreans were a mysterious and somewhat eccentric order: they worshipped numbers, believed in reincarnation, had strange rituals and eating habits, and remained individually anonymous by signing the symbol of the Pythagorean brotherhood (a pentagram) to everything they wrote or discovered.

pentagram

Over the years, Pythagoreans made enormous contributions to mathematics. Their name lives on today in the famous Pythagorean Theorem.

Pythagorean Theorem

The sum of the squares of the 2 small sides of a right triangle equals the square of the hypotenuse of that same triangle.

$$(a^2 + b^2 = c^2)$$

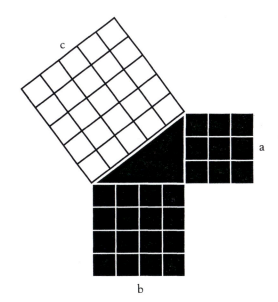

It is not known whether Pythagoras, himself, first proved this theorem or whether the proof must be more broadly attributed to the Pythagorean order. Although the Society of the Pythagoreans was communal in structure, with knowledge and property being held in common, it was their practice to credit all important findings to their leader, regardless of who actually made them.

Because of this practice, it is not clear whether Pythagoras or his society initiated the first scientific study of musical scales. Regardless, Pythagoras was clearly involved and is typically credited. This study proved that plucking two strings of equal tension, with one of them being half the size of the other, produced tones exactly an octave apart. In addition to the musical significance of this study, it also generated what are believed to be the first recorded facts in mathematical physics.

The Pythagoreans prospered and gained considerable political clout, but the mysticism and secretiveness of the order engendered the suspicion of the local population. A revolt in the region destroyed the buildings of the academy, causing the society to disperse. Pythagoras is variously reported to have burned to death with the buildings, or to have fled only to be murdered later. He is believed to have lived to the age of 75 or 80.

The society, though scattered, lived on for at least a century and produced other important mathematical works. Most of the material in the first two books of Euclid's *Elements* is believed to have been Pythagorean in origin. One of the most brilliant of the

Pythagoreans, Archytas, not only wrote extensively on the subject of solid geometry, but also authored a treatise entitled *On Music*. He was one of the earliest in a long line of mathematicians who also wrote on the subject of music.

Around the year A.D. 100, Nicomachus, described as a neo-Pythagorean, produced definitive mathematical documents entitled *Introduction to Arithmetic* and *Introduction to Geometry*. Although he is considered historically to have been a mathematician and philosopher, he also wrote *Introduction to Music* and *A Handbook of Harmonics*. Nicomachus defined arithmetic as absolute quantity and music as relative quantity, and wrote about the superiority of the Pythagorean integer ratios in music theory.

Ptolemy (c. A.D. 100–165) was perhaps the greatest astronomer and geographer of ancient times. His theories on astronomy (chief among them was the theory that the earth was the center of the universe) prevailed for 1,500 years, until the time of Copernicus. He is also considered to be one of the most important of the ancient writers on music. In *Harmonics* he expressed the belief that although the ear played an important role in matters of musical judgment, he, too, considered the Pythagorean integer ratios to be superior for creating musical intervals.

Boethius, who lived around A.D. 500, was the foremost mathematician of ancient Rome and the author of mathematical textbooks that were used for centuries. He is best known for his books on arithmetic, geometry, and astronomy, but he also wrote *The Principles of Music*, interpreting the earlier works on the subject by Nicomachus, Ptolemy, and Euclid.

There is a dearth of information about math and music during the Middle Ages (500 –1500); but since then there have been innumerable mathematicians who have extended their inquiries into music. Johannes Kepler (1571–1630) was a German astronomer and mathematician whose three laws of planetary motion contributed enormously to Sir Isaac Newton's discovery of universal gravitation. Recognizing that the planets revolve around the sun, he further refined the theory of the "music of the spheres" to suggest that the planets produce different sounds because of their varying degree of velocity, and that velocity is determined by size of orbit and by the distance from the sun. He believed that if the mass and velocity of a spinning object were known, it would be possible theoretically to

Boethius   Pythagoras

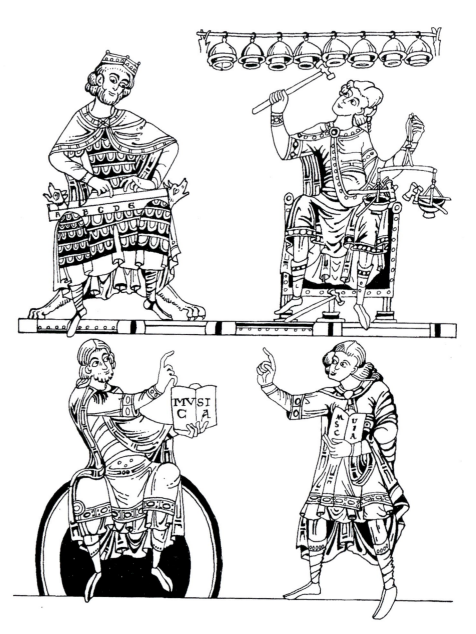

Plato   Nicomachus

calculate its fundamental pitch. He went so far as to develop little tunes for the planets known to exist at the time, which look like this in contemporary notation:

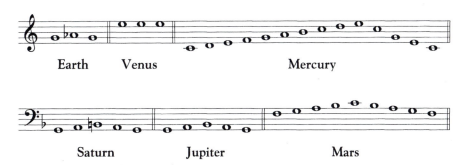

Father Marin Mersenne (1588–1648) was a number theorist best known for his work with the so-called Mersenne Primes, which are prime numbers that can be expressed in the form $2^n - 1$. He helped popularize equal temperament, and a method he devised of tuning by beats is still in use today. Galileo is known to have worked with Father Mersenne in his musical investigations.

Leonard Euler (1707–1785) was a Swiss mathematician who published *A New Theory of Music*, in which he analyzed the vibrations of bells and drums. The result of his work was extended to organ pipes by another Swiss mathematician, Daniel Bernoulli (1700–1782), a professor of mathematics at the University of Basel and a member of the mathematically prominent Bernoulli family.

THE MANY COMMONALITIES between math and music result in other "human intersections" of the two disciplines. Consider, for example, the fact that more child prodigies have been identified in the fields of math and music than in anything else. Some investigators have suggested that this is because the interpretation and manipulation of symbols is significant in both of these endeavors, and prodigies in both can infer a lot from relatively few examples. Social science, on the other hand, depends on an accumulation of considerable knowledge along with analysis thereof—and sufficient years in which to accomplish this. Few writers have ever been recognized as true child prodigies. Artistic prodigies are rare. Athletic precocity depends primarily on physical development, which is related to years of growth, as well as years of practice and skill development.

Though there is increasing scholarly interest in the field of *child prodigies*, a universally accepted definition remains elusive. A "highly talented child" or "a person who performs at or near the level of a professional at a very early age" are among the definitions being used. Harvard University psychologist Howard Gardner, in his studies of multiple intelligences, has observed that musical talent is usually the first to emerge and has speculated that musical ability does not seem to require as much experience in the real world as other skills. It would seem that mathematics is also somewhat less experiential and more instinctive in nature.

Historically, the two most prominent mathematical prodigies are Blaise Pascal and Karl Gauss.

Blaise Pascal   Karl Gauss

Pascal was born in France in 1623. His father did not allow him to study math before the age of twelve, so as a youngster he invented mathematics on his own, and taught himself geometry by the time he was twelve. At age 16, he attracted the attention of the great mathematician René Descartes by writing an authoritative book, *The Geometry of Conics*.

Gauss was born in Germany in 1777. When he was only three years old he corrected a computational error his father had made while working on his employee payroll. One day when Gauss was in third grade, his teacher (wanting some time to himself) told the class to add the numbers from 1 to 100. Almost instantly Gauss determined the answer. He noticed that pairing the numbers from the outside in—that is, pairing 1 with 100, 2 with 99, 3 with 98, and so on—produced the same sum, 101. He then multiplied that sum by the total number of pairs, 50. This is popularly known as "Rainbow Addition."

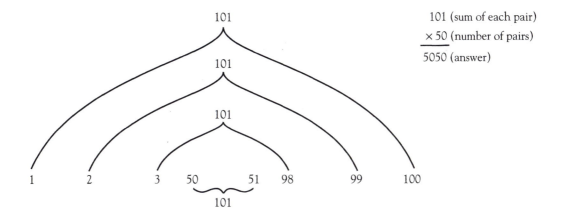

$$\begin{aligned} 101 \text{ (sum of each pair)} \\ \times\, 50 \text{ (number of pairs)} \\ \hline 5050 \text{ (answer)} \end{aligned}$$

Wolfgang Amadeus Mozart and Yehudi Menuhin are probably the two most well-known musicians commonly recognized as having been child prodigies.

Wolfgang Amadeus Mozart   Yehudi Menuhin

Mozart was born in 1756 in Salzburg, Austria, the son of a respected violinist and composer. He played the harpsichord at the age of 3, began composing music at the age of 4, and learned to play the violin when he was 6 years old. People were amazed at the extraordinary musical abilities possessed by one so young, so his father took him on tours throughout Europe to show off his "wonder child." From the time Mozart performed for the Empress of Austria at age 6, he spent many months a year traveling and performing for wealthy aristocrats everywhere. By age 15 he had written over 100 works. He is known to have liked billiards and chess, games with mathematical overtones.

American violinist Menuhin is regarded as the best known example of a single-purpose prodigy in the twentieth century. Born in New York in 1916, he began to study violin at the age of 5 and performed with the San Francisco Symphony Orchestra when he was only 7 years old. Critics at the time marveled at his technical virtuosity and uncanny understanding of the great works he performed.

AN INTERESTING STUDY conducted at the California State University in Fullerton, California, in the interest of finding an accurate predictor of academic success in music courses inadvertently highlighted a subtle relationship between math and music. A large battery of tests was used, most of which were music-based, except for the math and verbal sections of the Scholastic Aptitude Test (SAT®) (published by the Educational Testing Service in Princeton, New Jersey). Findings clearly indicated that the most reliable predictor of success in freshmen classes on music theory was the math component of the SAT. This finding is especially remarkable when one considers the significantly musical nature of all the other tests and the musical backgrounds of the examinees.

It seems appropriate here to mention the work of Zoltan Kodály in Hungary in the early 1900s. He is the founder of the Kodály Method of Music Education used worldwide today, based largely on the pentatonic (five-note) musical scale and Hungarian folk songs. His primary singing schools are credited with the high level of musical literacy in present-day Hungary. The Hungarian Ministry of Education allowed the continuation and expansion of these music-based schools because of the unexpected benefits the intense daily music instruction had on other academic areas—particularly mathematics. Hungarians attributed this to the theory that disciplines having common elements are mutually affected by changes in either.

JOSEPH SCHILLINGER is a prominent example of a teacher of both disciplines. He was a professor of both mathematics and music at Columbia University in the 1920s. He felt that all great works of music were constructed according to exact principles, and he effectively reduced musical composition to mathematical formulas. He once showed that a composition similar to Bach's could be manufactured by tracing the fluctuations of a *New York Times* business curve on graph paper and then translating the units of the graph into proportionate melodic and harmonic intervals. His most illustrious student was George Gershwin, and his mathematical system of composition is said to have figured prominently in Gershwin's famous opera, *Porgy and Bess*.

The life of M. Georges Cuisenaire represents another bridge between math and music. He invented Cuisenaire rods, which are used worldwide today to teach elementary mathematical concepts. He was trained as a composer at a conservatory in Belgium in the early 1900s. He began his educational career teaching music, though he later became an administrator. As an elementary school principal, he sought a method of teaching math concepts that children would enjoy as much as they enjoyed learning music from him. He conceived the idea of expressing numbers in color; since notes in music are based on specific mathematical intervals, these could be expressed by using colored rods of varying dimensions. He then amplified this idea and applied it to more general mathematical relationships. The rods are popular today as a manipulative way to teach math concepts. Some music teachers use them as a concrete way to teach counting in music. The colors of the rods and their lengths represent a double visual link to the numbers they represent.

Cuisenaire rods

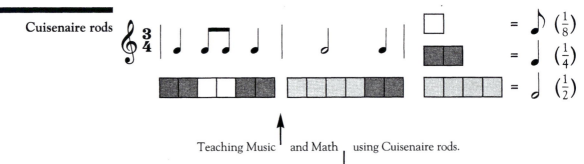

Teaching Music and Math using Cuisenaire rods.

$\frac{1}{8} = \frac{1}{4}$ of $\frac{1}{2}$ $\frac{3}{8} = \frac{3}{4}$ of $\frac{1}{2}$ $\frac{1}{8} = \frac{1}{2}$ of $\frac{1}{4}$

For many people today, both mathematics and music play important roles in their lives. It is not uncommon in many institutions and communities to find people who make significant contributions in both fields.

Examples might include a high school geometry teacher who plays keyboards in a rock band on Saturday nights or a scientist who conducts a recreational community chorus. It's common knowledge that musical support personnel in schools and colleges frequently emerge from the math and science departments, and that many of the best amateur musicians are applied mathematicians. Consider, for example, Hungarian-American physicist Edward Teller, who is also an accomplished pianist. Dr. Albert Schweitzer, a famous medical doctor, was equally famous as an organist and world-renowned authority on Bach. German astronomer Caroline Herschel, the first woman to discover a comet, began her professional life singing oratorios as a soprano soloist in England. Donald Knuth, a preeminent scholar of computer science, is an accomplished organist and composer. Albert Einstein, the brilliant scientist who, among other things, formulated the Theory of Relativity, was an excellent violinist. Curiously enough, however, when French violinist Jacques Thibaud was asked how he enjoyed playing quartets with him, Thibaud replied that Einstein was a good violinist but, unfortunately, couldn't count!

Albert Einstein   Einstein's house in Bern

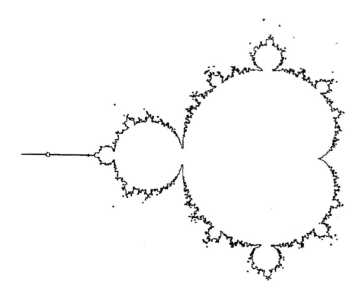

CHAPTER 8

THE CURIOSITIES

THERE ARE MANY weird, wild, and wonder-filled ways in which math and music relate to one another. Consider, for example, the story about popular singer Mariah Carey's hit song, "Someday," that ends on a high, loud note. One of her fans kept playing the song over and over again, and that final note made her automatic garage door keep opening and closing! Surely the math inherent in that music (pulsating waves, frequencies, beats, or decibels) figures prominently—however mysteriously—in such a phenomenon.

For curious links between math and music, the subject of **Fibonacci numbers** provides endless examples. These numbers are members of an infinite sequence named for a medieval mathematician, Leonardo of Pisa, who wrote under the pen name *Fibonacci*. He lived around A.D. 1200 and is important historically for having been the first person to formalize in writing the suggestion that Western civilization replace the awkward Roman numerals (I, V, X, and so on) with Hindu-Arabic numerals (1, 2, 3, and so on). He was also the first person to write down a unique sequence of numbers that are needed to answer a math problem he invented about the hypothetical breeding of rabbits. Centuries later, the sequence of numbers was named after him.

The first number in the Fibonacci sequence is 1, and each subsequent number is the sum of the previous two. Since there is only one number to start, adding 1 to nothing, which precedes it, produces another 1. Since each number in the sequence is the sum of the previous two numbers, it is now quite easy to build. The third number is 2, the sum of 1 and 1. The fourth number is 3 (2 + 1), the fifth number is 5 (3 + 2), and so forth. Following is the beginning of the Fibonacci sequence of numbers:

0+1	1+1	1+2	2+3	3+5	5+8	8+13	13+21
1,	1,	2,	3,	5,	8,	13,	21,	34,...

Clearly, Fibonacci numbers go on indefinitely. They form a fascinating sequence that has been studied over the years by mathematicians, artists, botanists, philosophers, stock market analysts, astronomers, physicists, computer programmers, poets, zoologists, and musicians because of their appearance in and applications to so many diverse fields.

Fibonacci numbers appear in a variety of places. Consider the keyboard of the piano: an octave is made up of 8 white keys and 5 black keys, the black keys are positioned in groups of 2 and 3, and there are 13 keys altogether in the octave. These are the first six Fibonacci numbers.

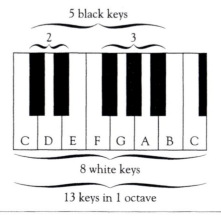

5 black keys

2   3

C | D | E | F | G | A | B | C

8 white keys

13 keys in 1 octave

A **Fibonacci ratio** is any Fibonacci number divided by one adjacent to it in the series. For example, 2/3 is a Fibonacci ratio, as are 5/8 and 8/13, and so on. The further along in the sequence that the ratios are positioned, the more similar to each other they become; they also become more exactly equivalent to the three-digit decimal fraction 0.618. . . . (The reciprocals of these fractions are, of course, greater than one; they converge to the decimal 1.618. . . .)

$$
\begin{aligned}
1/1 &= 1.000000 \ (+) \\
1/2 &= 0.500000 \ (-) \\
2/3 &= 0.666666... (+) \\
3/5 &= 0.600000 \ (-) \\
5/8 &= 0.625000 \ (+) \\
8/13 &= 0.615384... (-) \\
13/21 &= 0.619047... (+) \\
21/34 &= 0.617647... (-) \\
34/55 &= 0.618181... (+) \\
55/89 &= 0.617977... (-) \\
89/144 &= 0.618055... (+) \\
144/233 &= 0.618025... (-) \\
233/377 &= 0.618037... (+)
\end{aligned}
$$

The proportion that these ratios (in either fraction or decimal form) represent is considered by many to have a certain eye-appeal, balance, beauty. Because it is universally regarded as being quite special, it has come to be called the **golden proportion.**

0.618   1.000

Anything that is divided along this proportion is not static, even, or geometrically symmetric. Rather, it seems to have a flow to it, or a quality known as **dynamic symmetry.** The proportion can be found, for example, in the following geometric figures:

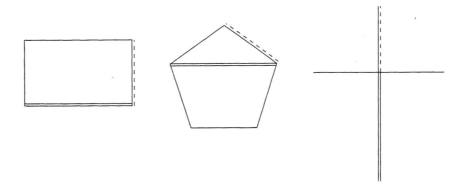

The golden proportion is also found in nature:

Norway spruce

Because of its aesthetic appeal, the golden proportion is used widely in art and architecture. Areas are divided to achieve the golden proportion in order to create a beautiful, balanced composition or construction. Fibonacci numbers are often used for that purpose because they are an easy way to determine the golden proportion.

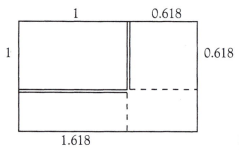

Example of how Fibonacci units can be used to achieve the golden proportion.

It seems that what is visibly beautiful is also audibly beautiful; the golden proportion clearly operates in music, especially in musical composition. For example, the number of measures in an entire composition might be a Fibonacci number. In that way, the period of time the composition represents can be subdivided into critical musical events—simply by making them last for a lesser Fibonacci number of measures.

144 measures
entire composition

		0.618	1
34 measures	55 measures	21 measures	34 measures
0.618	1		
Theme	Slow, soft	Fast, loud	Repeat of theme

The Hungarian composer Béla Bartók frequently employed this technique in the design of his compositions.

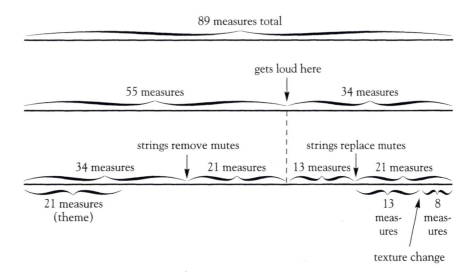

89 measures total

gets loud here

55 measures   34 measures

strings remove mutes   strings replace mutes

34 measures   21 measures   13 measures   21 measures

21 measures   13   8
(theme)   meas-   meas-
                                              ures   ures

texture change

First movement, *Music for Strings, Percussion, and Celeste,* by Béla Bartók. (Adapted with permission from Erno Lendvai, *Béla Bartók, An Analysis of His Music,* 28, 29.)

There are many ways in which Fibonacci numbers are used in musical composition. In some cases, this is clearly done by intent; in other cases, it will never be known whether or not a Fibonacci structure was intended or merely an accident of composition. Perhaps the composer simply wrote something that sounded right, or felt right. The positioning of the famous motto in Beethoven's *Fifth Symphony* is a good example:

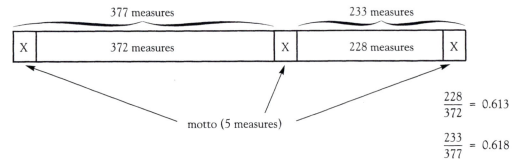

$$\frac{228}{372} = 0.613$$

$$\frac{233}{377} = 0.618$$

First movement of Beethoven's *Fifth Symphony*
divided into golden proportions by the motto.

Sometimes Fibonacci numbers are used to generate rhythmic change or to develop a melody line. Joseph Schillinger was an advocate of this technique. He developed the Schillinger System of Musical Composition used widely today. It involves leaping around the scale in interval units—usually half-steps—that are Fibonacci numbers (see the example on the next page).

Béla Bartók also used this technique in the development of his "Fibonacci Scale."

The numbers indicate half steps from C.

Fibonacci numbers can be found elsewhere in music. The proportions of some instruments are clearly "golden," as is the case with the violin. And sometimes golden proportions appear in an even less obvious way, as in the case of a strategically located bolt or other vital but obscure aspect of the engineering of the instrument. For example, the golden point (G) of the violin occurs at the intersection of two lines passing through the centers of the *f* holes.

KEY
1 = ½ step
1 = 1 step
1 = 1½ steps
and so on.

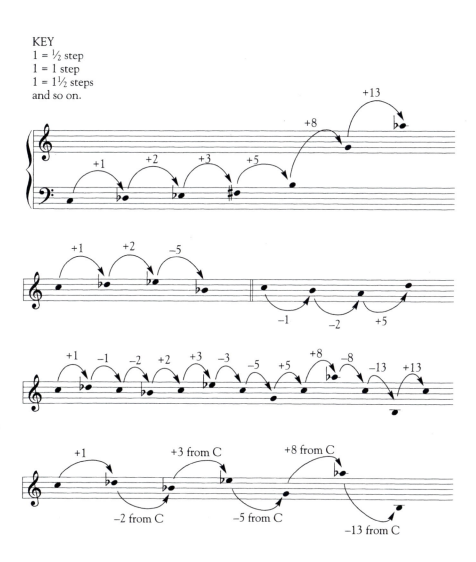

Examples of Fibonacci intervals between notes in melodies. (Adapted with permission from Joseph Schillinger, *The Schillinger System of Musical Composition*, 334, 337, 339, 341.)

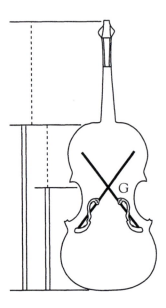

An examination of musical chords, especially beautiful ones, reveals yet another uncanny occurrence of Fibonacci numbers. The musical intervals considered by many to be the most dynamically pleasing to the ear are the major and minor sixths.

A major sixth, for example, might consist of C, vibrating at about 264 vibrations per second, and A, vibrating at about 440 vibrations per second. The ratio 264 to 440 reduces to 3/5, a Fibonacci ratio. An example of a minor sixth would be E (about 330 vibrations per second) and high C (at about 528 vibrations per second). That ratio, 330 to 528, reduces to 5/8, the next higher Fibonacci ratio. The vibrations of any sixth interval reduce to a similar ratio.

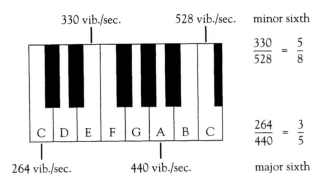

330 vib./sec.   528 vib./sec.   minor sixth

$$\frac{330}{528} = \frac{5}{8}$$

Just scale frequencies are used here, but any scale will reduce to the golden proportion.

$$\frac{264}{440} = \frac{3}{5}$$

264 vib./sec.   440 vib./sec.   major sixth

There is widespread speculation about the importance of Fibonacci numbers to the natural harmony that operates throughout the universe. The numbers themselves and the proportion they define not only look good to the eye and sound good to the ear, but also feel right aesthetically, are exact mathematically, and appear to be omnipresent!

THE MUSIC THAT is found in nature is often of mathematical interest. Consider, for example, the remarkably mathematically timed chirps of crickets. The number of chirps per minute is related to the temperature outdoors—the hotter the temperature, the greater the frequency of chirps. This explains why crickets do not chirp at all in the winter—it is simply too cold. The chirping of crickets can be reduced to the following linear equation:

$C = 4t - 160$, where C represents number of chirps per minute, and t represents temperature.

At 90 degrees Fahrenheit, there are 200 chirps per minute which can be somewhat difficult to count since they nearly flow together. At 72 degrees there are 128 chirps per minute, and at 50 degrees, there are only 40 chirps per minute. At 40 degrees or below, crickets are virtually silent.

The distance of an observer from a lightning strike can be accurately predicted by timing the delay of its thunder clap and applying a mathematical formula. Generally speaking, the time lapse (in seconds) between the lightning and the sound of the thunder associated with it is three times the distance (in kilometers) of the lightning from the observer. This also equates to five times the distance in miles. So the number of seconds it takes for lightning to be audible would be divided by three (for kilometers) or five (for miles) to determine its distance from the observer. However, thunder often has a certain rolling rumble to it, rather than an instantaneous clap. This is because lightning strikes are positioned somewhat vertically in the sky, and the sound created nearby reaches the listener before sound created farther away; the rumble is the sequential arrival of these sounds, which also vary in intensity and pitch.

The variety of sounds created by the wind are generally caused by the fact that as its speed increases, the frequency of vibrations increases, resulting in higher pitches. This is especially noticeable when wind whistles through small openings, such as between rocks and through holes in trees; a turbulence or some sort of vibration is established, the frequencies of which cause a whistle sound to rise or fall depending on how fast the wind is blowing.

Some of the sounds contributing to nature's symphony are generated in unusual ways. Cicadas, grasshoppers, and katydids rub the rough surfaces of their wings together to create vibrations that result in loud, raspy sounds. The wings of flies, bees, mosquitoes, and hummingbirds vibrate rapidly as they beat the air in flight, emitting light, characteristic humming sounds. The ruffed grouse beats its wings more slowly, lower to the ground, and closer to the body, creating a heavy thump in the woods.

Bats produce short, high-frequency sounds as they fly, the echoes of which help them determine the direction and distance of objects in the area. This method of navigating is known as *echolocation*. These sounds are **ultrasounds** and are inaudible to humans, since the frequency is above 20,000 vibrations per second. To gain a better understanding of ultrasounds, consider adding three more octaves at the high end of a piano keyboard; the highest one would get into the ultrasound range and could not be heard by humans.

Elephants, on the other hand, emit some low-frequency sounds that are beneath the range of human hearing. If one more octave were added to the low end of a piano keyboard, the lower notes would get into this **infrasound** range, below 20 vibrations per second. Elephants can hear these sounds—a fact that is critical to the survival of the species. Such sounds can travel enormous distances and alert other elephants to the availability of water or to existing dangers. A female elephant that is ready to mate has an effective, half-hour long infrasound song that draws receptive males from a radius of miles around. Humans can hear none of this—from any distance.

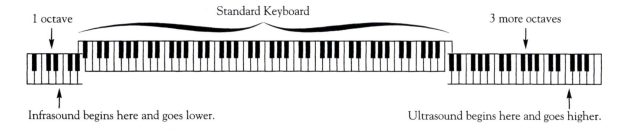

1 octave

Standard Keyboard

3 more octaves

Infrasound begins here and goes lower.

Ultrasound begins here and goes higher.

The earth itself is believed to be a constant source of infrasound. Mountains, for example, give off characteristic infrasounds that are believed to help migratory birds find their way. Earthquakes, volcanoes, ocean waves, and harsh weather also emit infrasounds, which can be heard by some animals but not by humans. This helps to explain why some natural disasters have been preceded by bizarre behavior on the part of household pets. Excessive activity by canaries and dogs has been reported just before volcano eruptions, earthquakes, and dam breakings. Relative to the planet Earth, perhaps there is something to the "music of the spheres" concept established in antiquity!

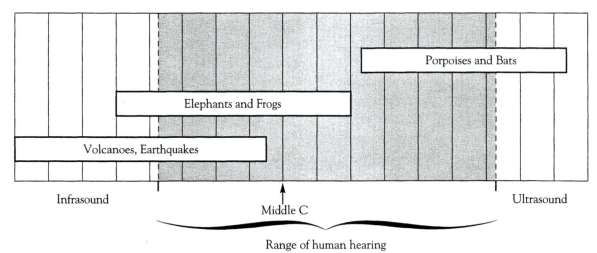

(each verticle bar = 1 octave)

Porpoises and Bats

Elephants and Frogs

Volcanoes, Earthquakes

Infrasound

Middle C

Ultrasound

Range of human hearing

Sounds—relative to human hearing

Another fascinating study is the singing of whales, aided in recent years by a popular recording, *Songs of the Humpback Whale*, featuring the strangely haunting cries, whoops, bellows, grunts, and roars of whale soloists. Whale songs are long and extremely complex, characterized in some cases by as many as ten distinct themes sung over and over again in perfect sequence. Amazingly, these themes are in the repertoire of every member of a whale herd, which can cover a territory the size of an ocean. Scientists have marveled over this and have speculated that the songs must be structured in some way so that whales can remember them and share them. Roger Payne, a professor of biology at Rockefeller University who has studied whales extensively, has suggested that they must "employ laws of composition remarkably similar to those of human music." Perhaps they use transformations, retrogressions, and inversions!

Possibly the most beautiful music in nature is that of birds. Bird songs vary enormously depending on species, gender, location, and season; their function is primarily courtship and the staking out of territory. Many songs are magnificent in their simplicity and beauty and have been emulated by great musical composers down through the ages.

There is often much more to bird songs than what is audible to the human ear, not only because the frequencies are sometimes out of the range of human hearing, but also because the speed of some songs does not allow for full reception of nuances and intricacies. A field biologist relates this story of taping the song of an indigo bunting. When he played it back at quarter speed, he was amazed at the detail that could not otherwise be heard. For example, he noticed that a little flourish at the end of the song sounded like the opening bars of "Reveille," a classic morning bugle call. As a joke, he whistled the remaining bars of "Reveille," spliced it onto the tape at slow speed, and played it back to other biologists at normal speed. No one noticed the addition!

AN INTRIGUING CORRESPONDENCE between musical sounds and colors has been observed over the years by various investigators. The frequencies of vibrations of musical notes ranging from G to F♯ can be aligned with the wavelengths of colors of the visible light spectrum as follows:

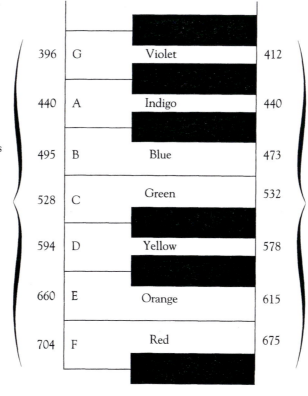

Sound frequencies in vibrations per second (using the Just scale, which represents a compromise between Pythagorean and equal-tempered tuning.)

396	G	Violet	412
440	A	Indigo	440
495	B	Blue	473
528	C	Green	532
594	D	Yellow	578
660	E	Orange	615
704	F	Red	675

Color wavelengths (the average of the accepted range) in nanometers.

The correspondence is further clarified when the colors and the notes are plotted together against a scale representing both nano-meters (used to measure color wavelength) and vibrations per second (used to measure musical pitch).

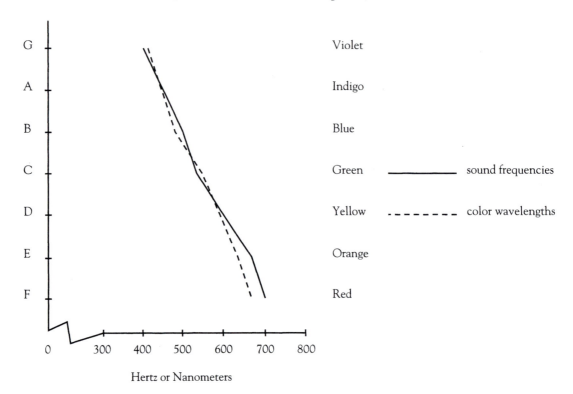

Hertz or Nanometers

The validity of this alignment has been disputed by both scientists and artists, with no definitive conclusions. At least part of the problem is the exactness of the relationships, which depends on the measurements used and the authorities invoked. The sound frequencies depend on which scale is used, and color wavelengths are sometimes indicated by a range of frequencies rather than a specific frequency; the exact color *orange* is subject to interpretation.

Nonetheless, the relationship is certainly tantalizing, and a proportionality clearly operates here. It has been suggested that the colors associated with some pleasing chords are themselves pleasing color combinations. At least one composer, Alexander Scriabin, incorporated dramatic colored lighting into the performance of his works. Beauty, however, whether visual or auditory, is in the eye or ear of the beholder.

ANOTHER INTERESTING RELATIONSHIP between math and music can be found in the art of film making. There are two basic methods of blending a musical score with a motion picture. In the first, the musical score is used to suggest a general mood, a place, a period of time, or a casual changing of these elements as they come and go. To do this, a composer simply needs to know the approximate length, order, and content of the scenes. In such situations the composer enjoys considerable freedom to develop a functional score, as there are no rigidly defined restrictions. In fact, the film maker sometimes accommodates the film to fit the written musical score, as necessary.

On the other hand, the purpose of music in a film might be to accompany and enhance very specific events as they take place. Music can magnify the impact of something scary or violent, for example, if it is timed just exactly right to the details of the scene. To do this, the composer must view the finished film and work out a "cue sheet" indicating critical events, shots, and their lengths. The number of frames dictates the length of a scene; since film is run at a specific number of frames per second, the timing of a scene can be calculated to a fraction-of-a-second.

As an example, consider a composition in four-four time being played at a metronome speed of 120 beats per minute, or 2 beats per second. At 4 beats per bar, a bar of music will last 2 seconds. At 24 frames per second (a standard in the industry), the equivalency in this case is:

48 frames of film = 2 seconds of time = 4 beats = 1 bar of music

or

24 frames of film = 1 second of time = 2 beats = 1/2 bar of music

The equivalency, of course, would differ using other metronome speeds, musical signatures, frame frequencies, or various combinations thereof.

It would be a mistake to suggest that the fine art of setting music to film can be reduced to a strictly mathematical formula. The technique, sometimes called "Mickeymousing" in reference to early efforts to set animation to music, draws significantly on emotional sensitivities, aesthetics, scientific acumen, and a sense of humor. Mathematics can, however, provide a critical link in this endeavor.

THROUGHOUT HISTORY, there have been various attempts to compose music using the rules and logical structure of mathematics. Composers have utilized specific techniques such as transformations and the calculus of probability, as well as more general ideas such as pattern, form, and repetition.

One compositional technique is to use an **algorithm**, which is simply a list of operations or set of rules for solving a problem.[18] One of the first to use a compositional algorithm was Guido D'Arezzo, a musical theoretician living in the early eleventh century. He proposed a method for putting any Latin text to music, which involved matching the vowels in the text with the notes in the double octave.

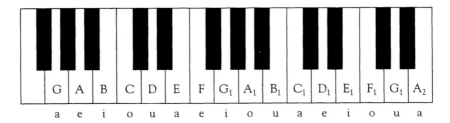

Notice that since there are four choices for a, and three choices each for e, i, o, and u, there are actually many solutions, or melodies, for a given line of text. In the end, the composer tinkers with the results of the algorithm and chooses the combination of notes that sounds best.

The previously mentioned serial music of Arnold Schoenberg and his students, Berg and Webern, is also algorithmic. One can write an algorithm to describe the process of choosing the order of the notes in the tone row. And once the notes are chosen, the rule is simply that no note can be repeated until all the notes in the row have been played, in order.

Since the 1950s, a **New Music** has arisen, inspired by the speed and accuracy with which computers can apply the steps in an algorithm and solve complex mathematical problems. Computers serve two functions in the world of New Music: they are used both to generate sounds, and to compose music. The complexity of the math and physics involved in computer sound generation prevents us from discussing it here, but we can take a quick look at some of the ways in which computers are used to write music.

Many algorithms for computer composition utilize the mathematics of chance and randomness. This is not a new idea. Mozart's dice game and others like it were created during the era that chance and probability were beginning to be explored by mathematicians. Many such games and aids for composers were produced, including one hilarious example, entitled *A Tabular System Whereby Any Person without the Least Knowledge of Musick May Compose Ten Thousand Different Minuets in the Most Pleasing and Correct Manner*, published by Peter Welcker in London in 1775. The element of chance in those compositions existed only on the level of choosing which measure, or which motif, came next. Because of the capability and accuracy of computers, the mathematics of chance involved in today's compositions is much more complicated. Composers use probability to control everything from pitch to rhythm to **dynamics** (louds and softs).

One of the first attempts at computer composition was made in 1957 by Lejaren Hiller, Leonard Isaacson, and Robert Baker. They used the Illiac computer at the University of Illinois to compose the *Illiac Suite for String Quartet*. The composers derived rules from various compositional styles and applied them to randomly generated notes, patterns of rhythm, and other musical properties.

This type of music is called **stochastic music.**[19] It is produced when an algorithm defining the style of the music is applied to a collection of random events (for example, a melody of randomly chosen notes). The rules may resemble existing compositional rules for a certain style of music (for example, baroque or jazz), rules employed by a certain composer (for example, Bartók or Gershwin), or rules inherent in a specific piece of music. The rules could even be completely unrelated to any music hitherto created.

For instance, the computer may use a random number generator to create a list of numbers, each of which is paired with a note on the keyboard. Then the computer checks the notes against the list of rules the composer/programmer has compiled. A rule might state, "there can be no interval larger than a fifth" or "an ascending sequence can be at most six notes long." The melody is finalized when all the rules have been satisfied.

A similar process may be employed in the creation of the rhythm by having the random number generator assign a duration to each note. Again, the composer can create a set of rules that the computer must check its assignments against, such as "no more than four sixteenth notes may occur in a row" or "all notes below middle C must be longer than an eighth note." The composer designs these rules to interact with the rules for the melody.

The composition of stochastic music, then, involves the interaction of the human and the machine. The composer creates the rules according to the style he or she is after in the piece of music, and then the computer generates the numbers (which correspond to the notes, the rhythm, and so on) and imposes upon them the composer's rules. And the composer can then fine-tune the results produced by the computer, if he or she wishes. It is important to note that since the composer/programmer creates the process, he or she could, theoretically, compose without the aid of the computer. But the math involved is sometimes so voluminous, it would take a lifetime of tedious calculation to get results a computer can get in minutes. The computer is a tool the composer uses to express his or her creativity.

However, computers are deterministic creatures, which means that the output they produce is completely determined by the input they are fed, such as the programmer's instructions, or algorithm. In other words, computers need to be told what to do, and need to be given the basic materials with which to do it. Therefore, there are certain limitations to what a computer can produce.[20] The music in the *Illiac Suite* is, reportedly, pleasant enough, but not particularly interesting, engaging, or beautiful. In fact, much of the stochastic music created since the 1950s has received the criticism either that it's boring or that it's too random to be beautiful.

Part of the problem with stochastic music is that it often lacks large-scale pattern. The rules imposed do create some pattern, but they often select a note based only on the characteristics of the last three or four notes. On a small scale, a given sequence of notes sounds musical, and is said to be strongly **correlated** (each note has a "memory" of what came before it). But that sequence won't necessarily be correlated to another sequence later on in the piece, resulting in an overall impression that the composition is rather random after all.

It turns out that the amount of correlation inherent in a composition has a definite effect on how musical it sounds. At one end of the spectrum of correlation, mathematically speaking, is **white noise** (see Chapter 3). Radio and television static are examples of white noise, as is the sound of rain hitting the roof.

This diagram of white noise sound waves suggests how one might write "white music"—a given note must be completely unre-

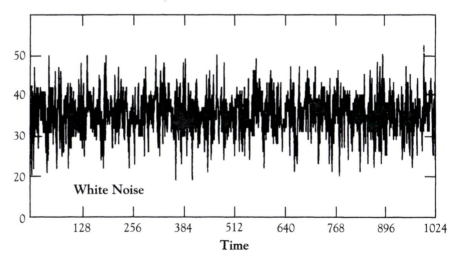

lated to (have no memory of) the notes that come before it. All one needs is a way to generate a random sequence of notes. One possibility is to use a dart board partitioned into seven sectors—one for each note of the C-major scale. Throw the dart, say, sixteen times to write a short "white song." Needless to say, the song will sound random and patternless, just like the sound of raindrops hitting the roof.

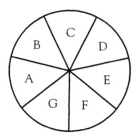

At the other end of the spectrum of correlation is **brown noise.** It is named after Brownian motion which, in physics, describes the random yet highly correlated "walk" of a dust particle suspended in a liquid whose molecules are pushing it about. Just as the particle of dust "remembers" exactly where it has been (it follows a continuous path instead of hopping around from spot to spot), a note in a "brown song" remembers the notes that come before it. The song, then, sounds highly correlated, and, therefore, highly predictable and uninteresting.

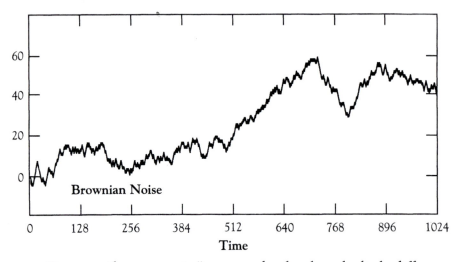

To create "brown music," arrange the dart board a little differently. Instead of using the names of notes, label the sectors with numbers ranging from −3 to +3, indicating the number of half steps up or down the next note should be. This way, a note depends entirely on the note that came before it.[21]

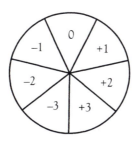

White music, then, is unstructured and random, and brown music is boring and over-correlated. Most stochastic music is too close to the white end of the spectrum to be truly musical, because the random number generators used have characteristics of white noise. It is natural to ask what type of noise lies midway between white and brown. Perhaps truly good music could be composed mathematically if its random elements were based on a compromise between these two ends of the spectrum.

Noise that lies between white and brown is sometimes called **flicker noise** in electronics. It is manifest in many ways in physics and nature, and is not always heard as a sound. For example, it has been found that sunspot activity, currents of nerve membranes, the growth of tree rings, and the flood levels of the Nile River all exhibit this type of noise; that is, these dynamic systems fluctuate over time with a pattern that can be described as flicker noise.

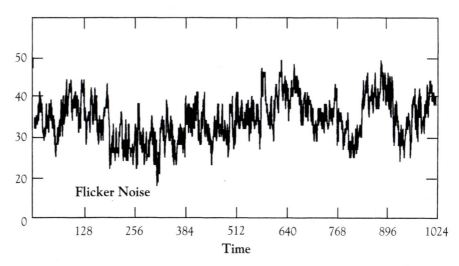

One of the most fascinating discoveries about flicker noise was made by Benoit B. Mandelbrot, the father of fractal geometry. He found that curves that trace out flicker fluctuations are scaling fractals. A **scaling fractal** is a geometric object that is infinitely **self-similar** (an example is presented below). That is, you can magnify it over and over again and you'll come up with the same pattern and detail, albeit on different scales. To get a feel for the self-similarity inherent in a fractal, study the creation of the infinitely complex border of what's known as the Koch snowflake, named after the Swedish mathematician Helge von Koch, who discovered it in 1904.

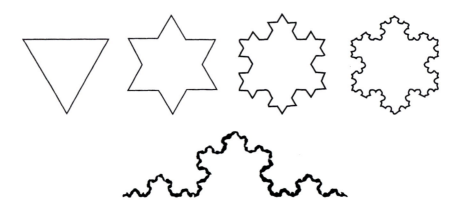

The natural world is composed of fractals that are the trails, or visual representation, left by the dynamic (continuously moving) systems that created them. A tree is fractal in nature—a single branch resembles the entire tree, a smaller twig resembles the branch, even the structure of the veins in the leaves exhibit the same branching process as the tree itself. Granted, the patterns at different scales are not exact replicas of one another, but the idea is the same. The patterns created by the rocks of a rugged coastline also repeat themselves at different scales—a snail crawling along the nooks and crannies of the rocks on the shore traverses a meandering path similar to the one you would take on a hike along the cliffs, which in turn is similar to the general outline of the coast viewed from an airplane. Natural fractals reach a point where the pattern (at the biological level, anyway) stops; however, in a true scaling fractal (for instance, the Koch snowflake), this detail continues ad infinitum.[22]

The concept of self-similarity so ubiquitous in nature has been employed in musical composition for centuries. Pieces are often organized into movements, which are further subdivided, and there is usually a theme or motif that repeats itself on various levels and scales. So it seems as though music shares some characteristics with the fractal patterns of nature. Sergei Prokofiev must have suspected this connection when he composed the score for Eisenstein's film *Alexander Nevsky*. In part, Prokofiev created the basis for the music by placing notes on the staff in positions that corresponded to the outline of the landscape!

If truly good music contains patterns that repeat at all levels, it's possible that the flicker noise exhibited by scaling fractals could provide a mathematical model for creating good music. Indeed, in the late-1970s two physicists, Richard F. Voss and John Clarke,[23] found in their research that nearly every kind of music, including Bach compositions, Hindu ragas, and Beatles songs, exhibits flicker noise. Music of this type has been called "pink music," because it lies in between brown and white music.[24] Following this discovery, Voss and Clarke did an extensive study in which they played white, pink, and brown music for hundreds of people, both musicians and non-musicians. Most people clearly preferred the pink music—it seems to have just enough randomness to be interesting, and just enough correlation over time to give a sense of large-scale pattern.

Granted, pink music (based on flicker, or pink, noise) isn't ideal, as you can see for yourself by playing through the pink song on the next page.[25] Even Voss' composition based on the fluctuations of the Nile's floodwaters, which exhibit flicker noise, doesn't approach the beauty of a Brahms intermezzo! However, most people in the study did call the pink songs "musiclike," attesting to some connection between the mathematical functions that describe pink noise and the patterns both in the natural world around us and in the music that we consider beautiful.

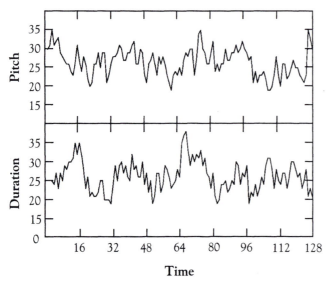

Pink Music

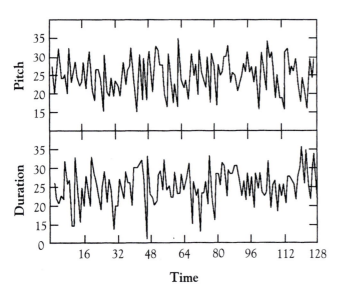

White Music

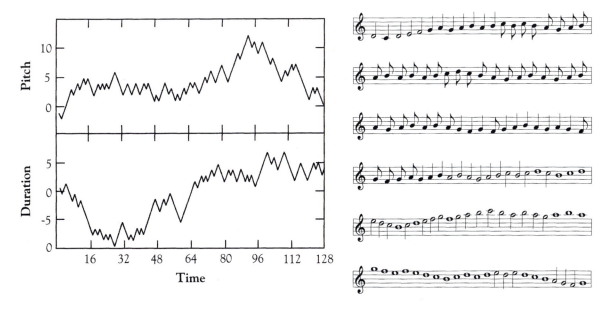

Brown Music

There is a definite interaction between art, science, and nature that becomes even more evident as discoveries like this are made. Over the years, philosophers, scientists, and artists alike have thought and written about this connection. Some have even come up with mathematical formulas that attempt to measure the aesthetic experience. However, one need only listen to a quartet of cellos playing a Bach chorale or to the liquid melodies of guitarist Stanley Jordan to be reminded of the expression, creativity, and life experience that go into composition and performance.

It is conceivable that there are certain characteristics that a creative work must have in order to be given that ambiguous label, *art*; for instance, a balance between complexity and simplicity, tension and resolution, chaos and order. It's doubtful, though, that we'll ever be able to completely quantify beauty with a simple formula, or that computers will ever create music as "good" as that created by humans.

THE NATURAL WORLD is teeming with dynamic systems. The weather, the delicate ecology of a Costa Rican rain forest, the stock market, the migration of monarch butterflies, the slow evolution of a wind-carved sandstone cave, the traffic flow across the Golden Gate Bridge—all of these are dynamic systems that are, at some level, interacting with each other and with the rest of the universe.

Dynamic systems are prone to display behavior that varies from being predictably stable to unpredictably chaotic. The new science of chaos theory concerns the study of these systems, and represents an attempt to understand the natural world on a new mathematical level. The emphasis is on understanding the border region between chaos and order, the region of activity where a system suddenly erupts into utter disorder out of what may seem like perfect stability.

The fractals inherent in nature are the fingerprints left by the workings of dynamic systems, so it makes sense that they encompass a balance between order and disorder. It also makes sense that inherent in music are some of the same patterns of self-similarity, and some of the same criteria for beauty, such as a balance between tension and resolution. After all, the creation and interpretation of music are themselves dynamic processes.

As Gert Eilenberger, a German physicist, said, "Our feeling for beauty is inspired by the harmonious arrangement of order and disorder as it occurs in natural objects—in clouds, trees, mountain ranges, or snow crystals. The shapes of all these are dynamical processes jelled into physical forms, and particular combinations of order and disorder are typical for them."[26]

A true artist must not only have an understanding of this balance, of the interconnectedness of all things, and of the patterns inherent at the many levels of existence; he or she must also be able to express this understanding in a way that others can, in turn, relate to their own understanding of the same. It's not so much that art imitates life, but that art is an expression of an individual's life experience—an experience that is intricately connected to the experiences of fellow inhabitants of this planet.

Art that is beautiful resonates deep within the soul. Music, in all its abstract and ephemeral beauty, taps a profound well of emotion, spirit, and biological rhythm that mirrors the patterns in the world around us. Perhaps our brains are like dynamic systems leaving their fractal traces. Is it surprising, then, that the mathematics created by those very brains describes the dynamic system that is our universe? And is it surprising that the music created and enjoyed by those very brains allows us to entrain with the many-leveled patterns of that universe?

As we evolve, so does our understanding of the universe, and so do our mathematics and our music. Music always has been, and always will be, a way to express ourselves as part of the pattern that math so aptly describes. Music gives beauty and another dimension to mathematics by giving life and emotion to the numbers and patterns. Each of us dances to our own internal rhythm, but also to the polyrhythm created by the whole band. And sometimes we all come together on "the One."

The mountains are singing—can you hear them?

1.   Hart, 1990. p. 196.

2.   Hart, 1990. p. 143.

3.   Sine waves are generated by Simple Harmonic Motion (SHM). A force that creates SHM has two properties: its direction is toward the equilibrium (original) position, and its magnitude, or size, is proportional to the displacement from equilibrium. A mass suspended at the end of a spring is an example of a system that experiences SHM.

4.   Frequency and wavelength are related by a quantity called **velocity**. The velocity of an object tells both its speed (given by the magnitude, or absolute value) and its direction (given by the sign, negative or positive). The velocity of a wave is the product of its wavelength (number of units of distance per wave) and its frequency (number of waves per second); i.e., $v = \lambda f$.

The speed of sound is a constant 331.5 m/s at normal room temperature and pressure (although the speed is higher for solid and liquid mediums than for gaseous mediums, and for each degree rise in temperature, the speed increases by 0.61 m/s). So for sound traveling through air, a shorter frequency implies a longer wavelength, and vice versa.

5.   Actually, it's a bit more complicated. The loudness of a sound depends on the **sound intensity,** which is a measure of the power of a sound per unit area and is equal to the square of the amplitude. A sound intensity of $4 \cdot 10^{-12}$ W/m^2 (Watts per square meter) is called the threshold of hearing, and a sound intensity of 1 W/m^2 is called the threshold of pain, for obvious reasons.

Since these values are rather awkward, a logarithmic scale was introduced. A sound intensity of 10^{-12} W/m^2 is defined as an intensity level of zero **decibels (dB).** An increase of 10 dB corresponds to a tenfold increase in sound intensity. The scale looks like this:

Intensity (W/m²)	Intensity Level (db)	Example
10^{-12}	0	near threshold of hearing
10^{-11}	10	
10^{-10}	20	whisper
10^{-9}	30	
10^{-8}	40	inside a running car
10^{-7}	50	
10^{-6}	60	conversation
10^{-5}	70	
10^{-4}	80	noisy street corner
10^{-3}	90	
10^{-2}	100	rock concert
10^{-1}	110	
10^{-0}	120	threshold of pain

The human ear actually responds to different frequencies in different ways, so frequency also plays a roll in the loudness of a sound. The most sensitive range for most people is between 1,000 Hz and 5,000 Hz. Sounds with lower frequencies must have a higher sound intensity to be perceived as being as loud.

6. Since $v = \lambda f$, there is a relationship between the wavelengths of the individual harmonics. The first harmonic, with frequency f, has $v = \lambda f$. Since the velocity of sound in air is constant, the second harmonic must have the same velocity. Its frequency is $2f$, so its wavelength must be $\lambda/2$, so that $v = (\lambda/2)(2f) = \lambda f$. Likewise, the third harmonic must have wavelength $\lambda/3$, so that $v = (\lambda/3)(3f) = \lambda f$. So the harmonics of a complex tone have wavelengths, λ, $\lambda/2$, $\lambda/3$, $\lambda/4$, and so on.

Some interesting waves can be created using various combinations of harmonics. For example, adding harmonics 1, 2, 3, . . . with relative amplitudes 1, 1/2, 1/3, . . ., all in phase, produces a **sawtooth wave**, as shown on the following page.

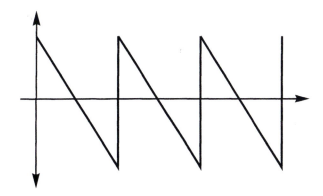

And adding harmonics 1, 3, 5, . . . with relative amplitudes 1, 1/3, 1/5, . . . , all in phase, produces a **square wave**:

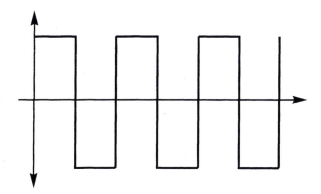

The famous mathematician, Joseph Fourier, proved that any periodic waveform with wavelength λ can be constructed by adding sine curves of wavelengths $\lambda, \lambda/2, \lambda/3, \ldots$ with appropriate amplitudes and phases. In other words, any periodic waveform with frequency f can be constructed by adding sine waves with frequencies $f, 2f, 3f \ldots$; that is, by adding the harmonics of the fundamental waveform. **Synthesis** is the process of adding partials to get the complex vibration or wave, while **analysis** is the process of breaking a wave down into its components.

7.   The proof is by contradiction. Assume the ratio of the side to the diagonal of a square is expressible as $p:q$ and we can write the ratio so that p and q are relative primes; i.e., $p:q$ is irreducible. The area of the square can be expressed in the normal way (p^2), or as the sum of two congruent triangles whose common base is the diagonal $(2[q/2 \cdot q/2] = q^2/2)$. Therefore, $2p^2 = q^2$. Then q^2 must be even, as must q; that is, $q = 2r$ for some r. But if q is even, p must be odd, otherwise $p:q$ would be reducible. However, $p^2 = q^2/2 = (2r)2/2 = 2r^2$, so p^2 must be even, and therefore p must be even! Since p cannot be both even and odd, we have derived a contradiction, and the original premise must be false. Therefore, we cannot always express the ratio of the side to the diagonal of a square as a fraction, and there exists a number that is **not** rational; hence, it is irrational. Q.E.D.

8.   van der Waerden, 1975. p. 92.

9.   Mersenne's rules:
      The frequency of a vibrating string is . . .
         1. inversely proportional to its length.
         2. proportional to the square root of the tension applied to the string.
         3. inversely proportional to its diameter.
         4. inversely proportional to the square root of its density.

10.   A is the **arithmetic mean** of X and Y if $A = (X + Y)/2$
       A is the **geometric mean** of X and Y if $X:A = A:Y$
       A is the **harmonic mean** of X and Y if $(1/A) = [(1/X)+(1/Y)]/2$

11.   Levarie and Levy, 1968. p. 212.

12.   Bower, 1967. p. 102.

13.   The first of the modern tuning reformers was the Spaniard Ramis de Pareja, who, in 1482, attempted to please both musicians and theorists with a compromise. He combined Pythagorean and Just tuning by using perfect fifths and four pure thirds in a way that produced simpler proportions than did Pythagorean tuning alone.

In 1518, Grammateus of Germany made a proposal to tune the white keys of a keyboard instrument using Pythagorean tuning, and then tune the black keys halfway between the white. In this temperament, the Pythagorean comma is divided equally between two of the fifths.

In the 1520s, Pietro Aron advocated what is called *meantone temperament*, a system with flattened fifths ($5^{1/4}$) and pure major thirds ($5:4$). It's called *meantone* because the tone C to D is exactly half of the pure third, C to E. Since $5^{1/4} = 1.49535...$, and $3:2 = 1.5$, there is a slight error, resulting in a gap between the notes of one of the fifths. This interval became known as the *quinte-de-loup*, or "wolf fifth," since it "howled like a wolf" instead of being harmonious. Musicians were restricted to playing in keys for which this fifth was not an integral part.

In 1533, Giovanni Maria Lanfranco put forth the first tuning rules for equal temperament: tune the fifths so flat that they sound off, and the thirds as sharp as one can stand. Mathematically, these instructions are incredibly vague, but they were useful to the musician. Many other tuning rules like this were given without precise mathematical description, and they were equally as useful to the musician.

In 1577, Francisco Salinas provided a precise mathematical description of equal temperament. Many geometrical, mechanical, and numerical approximations followed Salinas's, all of them incredibly mathematically complicated and often rather impractical for translation to the monochord and, therefore, not very useful to the musician.

In 1596, the mathematician Simon Stevin was the first European to actually construct a monochord using the ratio $2^{1/12}$. He expressed the radical belief that the irrational interval ratios were the true ratios, while the Pythagorean integer ratios were the approximations. Nevertheless, acceptance of equal temperament was still slow in coming, largely because the mathematics defining the tunings was too rigid.

14. An example of a rule for tuning by beats is that the listener should hear one beat per second for the interval of a fifth (because of the mathematics of beat frequencies) if it is tempered as it should be.

15. The German phrase for equal temperament, *die gleich-schwebende Temperatur*, is representative of how Bach and other musicians of the day utilized equal temperament. It means "the equally beating temperament," indicating a preference for tuning by beats over applying strict mathematics via a perfectly equally tempered monochord.

16. Paraphrased from McLeish, 1982.

17. Hart, 1990, p. 185.

18. The word *algorithm* comes from the Latin *algorism*, which was the name for the set of rules used to calculate with Arabic numerals.

19. Much stochastic music is based on Bernoulli's law of large numbers, which states that the more times a random process is iter-ated, the closer the resulting collection of data will be to conforming to statistical odds. This process implies an evolution toward stability, toward an end; hence, *stochastic*, from the Greek *stochos*, meaning "aim or goal."

20. For example, one criterion for an algorithm is "definiteness;" that is, each step must have a precise meaning—no fuzzy logic allowed! A recipe which includes the instruction "simmer until desired consistency is reached" is not an algorithm, because each chef has his or her own interpretation of "desired consistency."

21. You can introduce some order into the white and brown music by assigning different sizes to each sector of the dart board, and, therefore, different probabilities to each note or interval. For exam-ple, you may want the most common note to be middle C, with probabilities decreasing from there. Or you may want the interval of a whole step either up (+2) or down (−2) to be most common.

22. The smaller the scale, the longer the coastline becomes! A snail, crawling down the West Coast from Canada to Mexico would experience a much greater distance than an airplane flying the same route. It can be proven mathematically that the Koch curve encloses a finite area, but has infinite length.

23. Voss and Clarke, 1978.

24. The method for creating pink music is more complicated than that for white or brown. Gardner (1992) explains Voss' suggestions for creating music that is, for all practical purposes, pink music:

Use a purple, a green, and a yellow die, whose sum is at least 3 and at most 18, to create an 8-note tune from a scale of 16 adjacent notes on the piano. First, number the notes from 3 to 18, corresponding to the possible dice sums. Next, write the numbers 0 through 7 in binary, giving a color to each column.

number	purple	green	yellow
0	0	0	0
1	0	0	1
2	0	1	0
3	0	1	1
4	1	0	0
5	1	0	1
6	1	1	0
7	1	1	1

Now, toss the dice, and the first note of the tune will be the one corresponding to that sum. To get the second note, retoss only the dice that correspond to digit changes in going from "000" to "001;" that is, only the yellow die. The new sum consists of the original numbers on the purple and green dice, and the new number on the yellow die. To get the third note, retoss the green and the yellow dice, because both those digits change in going from "001" to "010." This time the sum consists of the original number on the purple die, and the new numbers on the green and yellow dice. Continue finding the notes in this manner, tossing the dice that correspond to changes in digit. For example, to get the fifth note, you'd need to shake all three die, because all three digits change in going from "011" to "100."

The tune created is between white and brown (between overly random and overly correlated) because the different die contribute in different amounts. That is, the digits to the right in the binary in different amounts. That is, the digits to the right in the binary representation (the least significant digits) change often, while the digits to the left (most significant digits) don't change as frequently. As a result, the dice that correspond to the digits on the left have more effect on the sum because they stay the same for a longer period of time. For example, the purple die stays the same for four tosses in a row, so whatever number it shows contributes to the sum of four consecutive notes.

25. Voss and Clarke note that more tinkering with the basic mathematical structure of pink noise is necessary to make truly good music. For instance, if only the melody is based on pink noise, so much else (rhythm, harmony, dynamics, etc.) that goes into composition is being ignored. They suggest using pink noise sources on different structural levels, and introducing external composition rules.

26. Gleick, 1987, p. 117.

Albers, Donald and G. L. Alexanderson, eds. *Mathematical People: Profiles and Interviews*. Boston: Birkhauser, 1985.

Allman, William F. "The Musical Brain." *U.S. News and World Report* (June 11, 1990).

Ardley, Neil. *Mathematics, An Illustrated Encyclopedia*. New York: Facts on File Publications, 1986.

Aristoxenus. *The Harmonics of Aristoxenus*. Ed. by Henry S. Macran. Oxford: Clarendon Press, 1902.

Austin, Joe Dan. *Applications of Secondary School Mathematics*. Reston, VA: National Council of Teachers of Mathematics, 1991.

Ayensu, Edward S., and Philip Whitfield. *The Rhythms of Life*. New York: Crown Publishers, Inc., 1981.

Backus, John. *The Acoustical Foundations of Music*. New York: W. W. Norton & Co., 1977.

Bateman, Wayne A. *Introduction to Computer Music*. Melbourne: Krieger, 1980.

Bell, Eric T. *Men of Mathematics*. New York: Simon and Schuster, Inc., 1986.

Benade, Arthur H. *Fundamentals of Musical Acoustics*. New York: Oxford University Press, 1976.

Beranek, Leo. *Music, Acoustics, and Architecture*. New York: John Wiley & Sons, 1962.

Bergamini, David, and the Editors of LIFE. *Mathematics*. New York: Time, Inc., 1963.

Bierhorst, John. *A Cry from the Earth: Music of the North American Indians*. New York: Four Winds Press, 1979.

Bower, C. M. *Boethius' The Principles of Music: An Introduction, Translation, and Commentary*. Ann Arbor, MI.: University Microfilms, Inc., 1967.

Boyer, Carl B. *A History of Mathematics*. Princeton, NJ: Princeton University Press, 1968.

Briggs, John. *Fractals: The Patterns of Chaos*. New York: Simon and Schuster, 1992.

Burney, Charles. *A General History of Music*. New York: Harcourt, Brace, and Co., Inc., 1789. 2 vols.

Cajori, Florian. *A History of Mathematics*. New York: Chelsea Publishing Company, 1985.

Choksy, Lois. *The Kodaly Method: Comprehensive Music Education from Infant to Adult*. Englewood Cliffs, NJ: Prentice-Hall, 1988.

Collier, James Lincoln. *Practical Music Theory*. New York: W. W. Norton & Co., Inc., 1970.

Cook, Cynthia Conwell. *The Ages of Mathematics: Volume III—Western Mathematics Comes of Age*. Garden City, NY: Doubleday & Co., Inc., 1977.

Cook, Peter D. *The Ages of Mathematics: Volume IV—The Modern Ages*. Garden City, NY: Doubleday & Co., Inc., 1977.

Doczi, Gyorgy. *The Power of Limits*. Boston: Shambhala, 1981.

Ellis, Keith. *Number Power*. New York: St. Martin's Press, 1980.

Eves, Howard. *An Introduction to the History of Mathematics*. Philadelphia: Saunders College Publishing, 1983.

Fauvel, John, and Jeremy Gray, eds. *The History of Mathematics: A Reader*. London: Macmillan Press, 1987.

Finney, Theodore M. *A History of Music*. Westport, CT: Greenwood Press, Inc., 1976.

Gardner, Martin. *Fractal Music, Hypercards, and More: Mathematical Recreations from Scientific American Magazine*. New York: W. H. Freeman and Co., 1992.

Garland, Trudi H. *Fascinating Fibonaccis*. Palo Alto, CA: Dale Seymour Publications, l987.

Gleick, James. *Chaos: Making a New Science*. New York: Penguin Books, 1988.

Grout, Donald J. *A History of Western Music*. New York: W. W. Norton & Co., Inc., 1980.

Harrison, Carole S. "Relationships between Grades in the Components of Freshman Music Theory and Selected Background Variables." *Journal of Research in Music Education*, 38, no. 3 (Summer 1990).

Hart, Mickey, with Jay Stevens. *Drumming at the Edge of Magic: A Journey into the Spirit of Percussion*. New York: Harper Collins Publishers, 1990.

Hawkins, Sir John. *A General History of the Science and Practice of Music*. 2 vols. London: Novello, Ewer, and Co., 1875.

Heath, Sir Thomas. *A History of Greek Mathematics*. New York: Dover Publications, Inc., 1981.

Hirsh, Alan J. *Physics for a Modern World*. Toronto: John Wiley and Sons, 1986.

Hoppin, Richard H. *Medieval Music*. New York: W. W. Norton and Co., Inc., 1978.

Hurd, Michael. *The Oxford Junior Companion to Music, 2nd edition.* London: Oxford University Press, 1980.

Hutchins, Carleen Maley. *The Physics of Music: Readings from Scientific American.* San Francisco: W. H. Freeman & Co., 1948.

Josephs, Jess J. *The Physics of Musical Sound.* Princeton, NJ: D. Van Nostrand Co., Inc., 1967.

Kappraff, Jay. *Connections.* New York: McGraw Hill, 1991.

Levarie, Siegmund, and Ernst Levy. *Tone, A Study in Musical Acoustics.* Westport, CT: Greenwood Press, 1981.

Linn, Charles F. *The Ages of Mathematics: Volume II—Mathematics East and West.* Garden City, NY: Doubleday & Co., Inc., 1977.

Machlis, Joseph. *The Enjoyment of Music.* New York: W. W. Norton & Co. Inc., 1977.

MacLeish, Roderick. "Gifted by Nature." *Smithsonian Magazine* 14(12), 1984.

Mandelbrot, Benoit B. *The Fractal Geometry of Nature.* New York: W. H. Freeman and Co., 1982.

Mathews, Max V., and John R. Pierce, eds. *Current Directions in Computer Music Research.* Cambridge, MA: The MIT Press, 1989.

McClain, Ernest G. *The Myth of Invariance: The Origin of the Gods, Mathematics, and Music from the RG Veda to Plato.* New York: Nicolas Hays, Ltd., 1985.

McLeish, Kenneth and Valerie. *The Oxford First Companion to Music.* London: Oxford University Press, 1982.

Moffat, Michael. *The Ages of Mathematics: Volume I—The Origins.* Garden City, NY: Doubleday & Co., Inc., 1977.

National Geographic Society. *The Marvels of Animal Behavior.* Washington, D.C.: The National Geographic Society, 1972.

Newman, James R., ed. *The World of Mathematics.* Volumes 1–4. Redmond, WA: Microsoft Press, 1988.

Payne, Katharine. "Elephant Talk," *The National Geographic* (August 1989).

Pendarvis, Edwina, et al. *The Abilities of Gifted Children.* Englewood Cliffs, NJ: Prentice-Hall, Inc., 1990.

Plato. *The Republic.* London: Oxford University Press, 1945.

Reinthaler, Joan. *Mathematics and Music.* Norman, OK: Mu Alpha Theta, 1990.

Ridout, Theodore C. "Sebastian and the Wolf," in *School Mathematics Study Group, Mathematics and Music,* ed. William L. Schaaf. Stanford, CA: Board of Trustees, Stanford University, 1967.

Roads, Curtis, ed. *The Music Machine: Selected Readings from Computer Music Journal.* Cambridge, MA: The MIT Press, 1989.

Russcol, Herbert. *The Liberation of Sound: An Introduction to Electronic Music.* New York: Da Capo Press, Inc., 1987.

Struik, Dirk J. *A Concise History of Mathematics.* New York: Dover Publications, Inc., 1987.

van der Waerden, B. L. *Science Awakening I: Egyptian, Babylonian, and Greek Mathematics.* Princeton Junction, NJ: Scholar's Bookshelf, 1988.

Voss, Richard F. and John Clarke. "'$1/f$ noise' in music: Music from $1/f$ noise." *The Journal of the Acoustic Society of America* 63, No. 1 (January 1978): 258–263.

Warren, Dr. Fred, with Lee Warren. *The Music of Africa: An Introduction*. Englewood Cliffs, N.J.: Prentice-Hall, Inc., 1970.

White, Harvey E., and Donald H. White. *Physics and Music: The Science of Musical Sound*. Philadelphia: Saunders College, 1980.

Willson, Robina Beckles. *The Voice of Music*. New York: Atheneum, 1977.

Zaslavsky, Claudia. *Africa Counts: Number and Pattern in African Culture*. Brooklyn, NY: Lawrence Hill Books, 1979.

Pythagorean, 51, 56–65
Reformation-era, 142–143
theory, 37–63
Twelve-note tone rows, 77–79

Ultrasound, 121, 122
Unison, 35
Universe, music in, 98, 101, 103

Velocity
frequency and wavelength and, 139
planetary music and, 101, 103
Vibration
color and, 124
Fibonacci ratio and, 118
pitch and, 28–29
sources of, 88
wave direction and, 21–24
Villa-Lobos, Heitor, 86
Violin, 89
golden point of, 116
Violin string
See also String, sound produced by
harmonics and, 34
longitudinal wave transmitted by, 25
partials created by, 32
transverse wave created by, 22–23
Vocal cords, 92–93
Voice, as musical instrument, 92–93
Voss, Richard F., 133, 145, 146

Waveform, 26
flute vs. guitar, 26–27
resultant, 29–32
Wavelength, 27, 28
harmonics and, 140
tone and, 29

velocity and, 139
Wave motion, 20–26
Waves, 20
amplitude of, 27, 28
crests and troughs of, 20, 21
infrasound emitted by, 121
longitudinal, 23–26
partials, 32
in phase/in opposite phase, 30
quantity measures, 27–28, 139
rhythm created by, 6
sawtooth, 140–141
sound, 25–27
square, 141
synthesis vs. analysis of, 141
transverse, 21–23, 26
Weather, 121, 136
Welcker, Peter, 127
The Well-Tempered Clavichord, 65, 79
Whales, 122
When the Saints Go Marching In, 70
White music, 129–130, 131, 134, 144
White noise, 34, 129
Whole note, in $\frac{4}{4}$ measure, 8
Whole rest, 8
Whole step, 38, 39
Whole tone, 54
in diatonic scale, 54–56
Wind, sounds created by, 120
Wind instruments, 90–93
spacing of finger holes in, 45
Woodwinds, 90–91
Written music, 7, 44

Yankee Doodle, transposition in, 71–72